The DARVO Playbook

Recognize the Deny, Attack, Reverse Tactic, Trust Your Own Reality, and Take Back the Conversation with a Manipulator

AF866653

Arnold Wellington McLean

The DARVO Survival Guides, Book 1

Copyright

Disclaimer

This book is for information and education. It is not therapy, counseling, medical advice, or legal advice, and it is not a substitute for care from a qualified professional. Reading it does not create a therapeutic or professional relationship. If you are in danger, or if you are struggling with your mental health, please contact a licensed professional or your local emergency services.

The people in this book are fictional composites. Every case study is invented to illustrate a pattern, built from the kinds of situations that show up again and again in this work. No character is a real, identifiable person, and any resemblance to a specific individual is coincidental.

The strategies here can help you understand and respond to a manipulation tactic. They do not guarantee any particular outcome, and they cannot change another person. What they can do is help you see more clearly and act with more steadiness.

First Edition

ISBN: 9798906782205

Staten House

Table of Contents

You've been DARVOed

You went in to say one clear thing. Something happened, it hurt, and you needed to name it. You had the sentence ready. And somehow, a few minutes later, you were the one apologizing. You were explaining your tone. You were defending your memory of an event you were certain about when you walked in. By the end, the thing you came to say had vanished, and in its place was a new question you had never meant to ask: what is wrong with me?

If you have lived that exact reversal, more than once, with the same person, this book is for you. What happened to you has a name. It is called DARVO, which stands for Deny, Attack, and Reverse Victim and Offender. It is a specific, documented manipulation pattern, first named by the psychologist Jennifer Freyd in her research on how people respond when they are confronted about causing harm (Freyd, 1997). It is not a mood. It is not a misunderstanding. It is a sequence, and once you can see the sequence, it stops being able to hide.

Here is the part that matters most on this first page. The confusion you felt was not a sign that you are too sensitive, too dramatic, or too difficult. The confusion was the point. DARVO is built to produce exactly the fog you walked out in. Researchers have found that when people are exposed to this tactic, they tend to blame themselves more and to see the person who was actually harmed as less credible (Harsey et al., 2017). In other words, the self-doubt you have been carrying is not evidence against you. It is evidence that a tactic worked the way it was designed to work.

You have probably already read a definition of DARVO somewhere. That is likely part of why you are here. The word is everywhere now, in articles and videos and comment sections, and almost all of it stops at the same place. It tells you what the letters stand for, tells you to stay grounded, and then leaves you standing in your kitchen with no idea what to actually say the next time it happens. This book is the other half. It is the part where you learn what to do.

So let me be candid about what this book is and what it is not. It is not a textbook, and it is not a long history of narcissism with your problem buried in chapter nine. It is not a sales funnel for a program you have to buy to get the real answers. It is a working playbook. You will learn to spot the three moves as they unfold. You will learn to steady your own body before you respond, because you cannot think clearly while you are flooded. You will get actual words, lines you can say and adapt, that hold your ground instead of handing it over. You will learn to keep a simple record that protects your memory from being rewritten. And you will learn to handle the version of this that goes public, when the other person tells everyone their story first.

There is one more thing this book will ask of you, and I want to name it now so it does not surprise you later. Somewhere in these pages you will do a clear-eyed self-check. Not every hard conversation is DARVO. Sometimes people just disagree. Sometimes you owe an apology and a manipulator is also twisting the moment, both at once. A book that told you that you are always right and always the victim would be lying to you, and it would leave you worse off, not better. This book will help you tell the difference, because your credibility, with yourself and with everyone watching, depends on getting that difference right.

Read the early chapters in order, because recognition comes first. After that, keep the response chapters within reach and return to them before the conversations you know are coming. You do not need to master all of it today. You need one thing to be true by the end of this Introduction, and it already is: what happened to you is real, it has a name, and it can be answered. Let's begin with the name.

Action step: Before you turn the page, write down one recent conversation that left you feeling like the problem when you did not start out that way. A few lines is enough. You will use it as your own worked example as the book goes on.

Chapter 1: The Tactic with a Name

Avelis had rehearsed it in the car. She was thirty-eight, and she had spent most of those years being the reasonable one in her family, the one who smoothed things over, so this small act of directness felt enormous. Her sister had promised, again, to help with their father's care and had disappeared the moment it was time to actually show up. Avelis was tired in a way that had stopped being about sleep. She only wanted to say one sentence: I need you to do what you said you would do.

She got the sentence out. What came back did not touch it. "That is not what happened," her sister said first, with a certainty so flat that Avelis felt her own memory wobble. Then, before Avelis could steady herself, the ground shifted again. "You have been impossible to deal with lately. Everyone has noticed. I have been walking on eggshells around you for months." And then, in a voice gone suddenly small and wounded, the final move. "I have been doing my best. I cannot believe you would attack me like this when you know how hard things have been for me."

Avelis apologized. She heard herself do it. She heard herself say that she knew things had been hard, that she had not meant to attack, that maybe she had been stressed and taken it out on her sister. She drove home replaying it, and the strange thing, the thing that kept her up that night, was that she could no longer locate the original problem. The broken promise had evaporated. What remained was a picture of herself as someone difficult and cruel, someone who ambushed a struggling sister over nothing. She had walked in holding a legitimate need and walked out holding a case against herself.

She did not have a word for what happened. That was the worst part. Without a word, it was just a feeling, and the feeling pointed straight back at her. If she had known one word, the whole night might have gone differently, not because the word is magic, but because of what a word does. A word lets you stand outside a thing and look at it. Without it, you are inside the fog, and inside the fog every road leads back to your own guilt.

The three moves, named

The word Avelis needed is DARVO. It stands for Deny, Attack, and Reverse Victim and Offender, and it names a specific sequence that people run when they are confronted about something they did (Freyd, 1997). Read her sister's three responses again and you will see the sequence exactly. That is not what happened is the Deny. You have been impossible, everyone has noticed is the Attack. I cannot believe you would attack me when you know how hard things have been for me is the Reverse, the moment the person who caused the harm becomes, in the space of one sentence, the one who has been harmed.

The order can shift, and the words change every time, but the structure holds. First a flat rejection of your reality. Then a strike at your character, your tone, your memory, or your motives. Then the flip, where they take the role of victim and hand you the role of offender. The content is endlessly adaptable. The machine underneath it is not. Once you have seen the three moves clearly, you start to catch them in real time, and catching them in real time is where all of your power lives.

Where the term comes from

DARVO is not a word someone coined for social media. It came out of research. Jennifer Freyd, a psychologist who studied how people respond to betrayal and to being confronted about harm, named the pattern in the late nineteen nineties (Freyd, 1997). What she was describing was not new behavior. People have been denying, attacking, and flipping the victim and offender roles for as long as anyone has been asked to take responsibility. What was new was giving that particular sequence a name, so that it could be studied, recognized, and taught.

Since then, researchers have looked at what DARVO actually does to the people on the receiving end. In one line of study, exposure to the tactic was linked to higher self-blame in the person who had been harmed, and to that person being seen as less believable (Harsey et al., 2017). Later work found that when observers watched someone use DARVO, it shifted how credible both parties seemed, tending to protect the person using it (Harsey & Freyd, 2020). This is the research underneath Avelis's terrible drive home. Her self-blame was not a personal weakness. It was the documented, predictable effect of a tactic that was working.

A script, not a diagnosis

Here is a distinction that will save you a great deal of confusion, so hold onto it. DARVO is a script, not a diagnosis. It is something a person does, not a category a person is. This matters for two reasons.

First, it keeps you grounded. You do not need to decide whether your sister, or your partner, or your manager is a narcissist, or has any particular disorder, to notice that they just ran the three moves. You are not diagnosing anyone. You are describing a behavior you can see, the way you might notice someone raising their voice. That keeps you on solid ground, because you are talking about what happened, not about what is wrong with someone's soul.

Second, it protects you from a trap. When you turn DARVO into a label for a whole person, you tend to either write them off completely or, more dangerously, decide that because they are a certain type, nothing you do matters, so you stop protecting yourself. Seeing DARVO as a script keeps your attention where it belongs, on the pattern in front of you and your response to it, which is the only part of this you can actually influence.

Anywhere a person can be asked to take responsibility, the DARVO script is available to them. It shows up between partners, between parents and grown children, between friends, between colleagues, in courtrooms, and in public life on the largest possible stage. The setting changes the stakes. It does not change the shape.

The same shape in a different room

To see how portable the pattern is, move it out of Avelis's family and into an office. Isoren, a project lead in their forties, raised a simple, documented concern with a colleague: a deadline had been missed, and it had cost the team a week. They said so plainly and privately. The reply arrived in three familiar beats. "I never got that timeline from you," the colleague said, though it sat in a shared calendar both of them could open. That is the Deny. "Frankly, people find you really hard to work with, and I have been trying to protect you from hearing that," they went on. That is the Attack, and notice the small gift wrapped inside it, the pose of someone doing you a kindness while they cut. Then the close. "I have been under enormous pressure, and now I am being blamed for everything. I do not know how much more of this I can take." That is the Reverse.

Isoren left the conversation apologizing for adding to the colleague's stress, which is a remarkable outcome for a person who began the conversation as the one holding the missed deadline. Nothing about the office changed the machine. The words were different from Avelis's sister, the setting was different, the relationship was different, and the three moves were identical. This is what it means to say DARVO is a script. Learn the shape once and you will recognize it in rooms you have not walked into yet. It is worth sitting with how strange that is. Two people who have never met, in a family living room and a corporate office, reached for the same three moves in the same order, because the moves are not really about the relationship. They are about escaping accountability, and the fastest route out of accountability turns out to look the same almost everywhere.

You may already feel a caution rising here, and it is a good one to trust. If three moves this simple explain so much, is there a risk of seeing DARVO everywhere, of slapping the label on every disagreement and every person who ever pushes back on you? Yes. There is. That risk is real, and it is important enough that a later chapter is devoted entirely to the rigorous self-check that keeps you from misusing this. For now, hold both truths at once. The pattern is real and worth learning to see. And not every hard moment is the pattern. Recognition means seeing DARVO when it is there, which also means being willing to see when it is not.

Why naming breaks the spell

There is a reason this chapter is about the name before it is about anything else. Naming a tactic while it is happening changes what the tactic can do to you. I call this the Naming Advantage: once you can name a manipulation tactic while it is happening, it loses much of its grip, because recognition pulls you out of the confusion it depends on.

Think about what confusion needs in order to work. It needs you to be inside it, reacting, scrambling to defend yourself, trying to answer three different accusations at once. The moment you can think the words this is DARVO, a small but decisive thing happens. Part of you steps back and becomes an observer. You are no longer only a participant being swept along. You are also a person watching a known pattern unfold, and a pattern you can watch is a pattern you can choose how to answer. This is consistent with what Freyd and her colleagues have argued about DARVO, that understanding the tactic is itself a form of protection against it (Harsey & Freyd, 2020).

There is also a quieter benefit, and it lands after the conversation is over, not during it. Most of the damage from DARVO is not done in the room. It is done in the hours afterward, when you replay the exchange and slowly talk yourself into being the villain of it. That replay is where self-blame hardens into belief (Harsey et al., 2017). When you have a name, the replay changes. Instead of what is wrong with me, the question becomes which of the three moves did they use, and the answer is right there in front of you. You are analyzing a pattern rather than prosecuting yourself. The name does not just help you in the moment. It changes the story you tell yourself for days after.

Naming does not make the other person stop. Let me be clear about that, because false promises are how a lot of these books lose your trust. Your sister will very likely run the same three moves next time. What changes is not her. What changes is you, standing outside the fog instead of lost in it, which is the difference between apologizing on the drive home and knowing, calmly and without needing anyone to agree, exactly what just happened.

Trying it on your own life

Recognition is a skill, and skills grow with reps. So let's start getting reps now, with small, low-risk actions you can take this week.

The first is almost embarrassingly simple, and it is the most important. Say the sentence out loud, alone, in a calm moment: "This is DARVO. Deny, attack, reverse victim and offender." Say it a few times until it feels available, until it is a phrase your mind can reach for under stress rather than a term you read once. You are building a handle you can grab in the dark.

The second uses the example you wrote down at the end of the Introduction. Take those few lines and go through them slowly. Where is the Deny, the flat rejection of what you raised? Where is the Attack, the pivot onto your character or tone? Where is the Reverse, the moment they became the wounded party? If you have colored pens, mark each move in a different color. If you do not, just label them in the margin. What you are training is the eye that catches the three moves, and on the page, at your own pace, that eye grows fast.

The third is a single line in a notebook or a note on your phone. Write today's date and one sentence: the pattern I keep meeting is called DARVO. That line is the first entry in something you will build later in this book, a simple record that will matter more than you might guess right now.

The fourth is about your body, and it is preparation for a skill we return to in depth later. The next time a conversation starts to tilt in the familiar way, before you try to say or do anything clever, just notice one physical signal. Maybe your chest tightens, your face goes hot, your thoughts speed up, or you go strangely blank. You do not have to fix it yet. You are only learning your own early warning system, because your body almost always registers the shift a beat before your mind names it. That beat is going to become useful.

A word about what to expect as you practice. Recognition rarely arrives as a clean lightning strike in the middle of the argument, at least not at first. More often it comes late, an hour afterward, when you suddenly think, that was the three moves again. That is not failure. That is the skill installing itself. The gap between the conversation and the recognition shrinks with reps, from the next day, to that evening, to the drive home, until one day it happens while you are still in the room. When it does, you will feel the ground change under you, and you will finally have the footing to respond. That response is what the rest of this book is for.

In a nutshell

What happened to Avelis, and what has been happening to you, is not a mystery and not a character flaw. It is a named tactic, DARVO, with three moves: deny the thing, attack the person who raised it, and reverse the roles of victim and offender until you are the one apologizing (Freyd, 1997). It came out of research, and that research shows the self-doubt it produces is the tactic working, not proof of your guilt (Harsey et al., 2017). DARVO is a script someone runs, not a diagnosis you have to make, and the single most useful thing you can do first is learn to name it in the moment, because the Naming Advantage pulls you out of the confusion the tactic depends on. You have the name now. Next, we slow the three moves down and take each one apart, so you can see them coming before they land.

Chapter 2: Anatomy of a Reversal

Vaelan replayed the fight so many times that he started to lose track of which version was real. He was forty-one, careful by nature, the kind of person who checked his facts twice before speaking. So when he told his partner that the money set aside for rent had been spent, he had already looked at the account three times. He was sure. He said it quietly, without accusation, because he did not want a fight. He wanted a plan.

What he got was a wall. The first thing his partner said was that the money had never been there, that Vaelan was confused, that he always got numbers wrong. Vaelan actually opened his phone to check a fourth time, which is the small tell he later learned to notice in himself, the reflex to prove a thing he already knew. Before he could find the screen, the conversation had moved. Now they were talking about how controlling he was, how he watched every dollar, how exhausting it was to live under that kind of surveillance. And then, somehow, his partner was crying, and Vaelan was the one holding a tissue box and saying he was sorry for making them feel watched.

He went to bed that night having apologized for raising a real and serious problem, with the rent still unpaid and the problem still unsolved. What haunted him was not only the outcome. It was that he could not point to the exact moment it turned. It felt like water. One second he was standing on solid ground and the next he was underwater and could not say when he had gone under. That is the feeling this chapter is going to fix, because the turn is not water. It has parts. It has an order. And parts you can name are parts you can see coming.

Slowing the tape down

DARVO happens fast on purpose. Speed is part of how it works, because a fast reversal does not give you time to hold onto the original point. So the first skill is to slow the tape down, to watch each move in isolation the way you might watch a single frame of a film that otherwise blurs past. Freyd named three moves, Deny, Attack, and Reverse Victim and Offender, and each one does a specific job (Freyd, 1997). When you can see the job each move is doing, the whole sequence stops feeling like weather and starts looking like machinery.

Let's take them one at a time, using Vaelan's night as our slowed film. Then we will look at why they tend to arrive in this order, and what the order is designed to accomplish.

Deny, the move that closes the door

The first move is denial, and it is usually flat. Not "I remember it differently," which is an opening for conversation, but "that never happened," which is the closing of one. Vaelan's partner did not say the money situation was complicated. They said the money was never there. The denial was total, and total denial is a signal, because reasonable disagreement almost always leaves a door open. Total denial slams it.

The job of the Deny is to make your reality the thing in question. Notice what it does to your attention. The instant someone flatly denies what you know to be true, part of you turns inward to check, to re-examine your own memory, to make sure. That turning inward is exactly the point. While you are busy auditing yourself, you are no longer looking at their behavior. The denial has moved the spotlight off the deed and onto your perception, and that is a move you can now recognize by its effect on you. When you feel the sudden urge to prove something you already know, you are almost certainly standing in front of a Deny.

Attack, the move that changes the subject

The second move is the strike, and its job is to change the subject from what they did to who you are. Watch how cleanly it works in Vaelan's story. He raised a fact about money. The Attack answered with a claim about his character, that he is controlling, that he surveils, that he is exhausting to live with. Nothing in that answer touches the rent. It does not need to. The Attack is not trying to win the argument about money. It is trying to end the argument about money by starting a different one, an argument about your worth.

There is a reason attacks land so hard and stick so long, and it is not that you are weak. Human attention is tilted toward threat and criticism. Negative information about ourselves tends to hit harder and linger longer than positive information, a pattern researchers have documented across many areas of life (Baumeister et al., 2001). A manipulator does not need to know that research to use it. They only need to know that if they hit your character, you will drop the ledger and pick up the wound, because that is what people do. The Attack weaponizes an ordinary feature of how your mind works.

Reverse Victim and Offender, the move that flips the roles

The third move is the flip, and it is the one that gives the tactic its terrible power. Having denied the deed and attacked your character, the person now takes the last open role, the role of the wounded party. Vaelan's partner cried. In that moment the person who spent the rent became the person who was hurt, and Vaelan, who had lost the rent, became the person who had done the hurting. The roles did not just blur. They swapped.

This is the move that produces the apology on the drive home, or in Vaelan's case the tissue box in his own hands. Once the roles are reversed, your own decency turns against you. You are a person who does not want to hurt anyone, so when you are cast as the one causing pain, you rush to repair it. You comfort them. You apologize. The Reverse takes your empathy, which is a good thing about you, and points it in the wrong direction, at the person who caused the harm rather than at yourself, who received it.

Why the order matters

The three moves can arrive in different sequences, and sometimes they overlap or repeat, but this order, deny then attack then reverse, is common because it builds. The Deny destabilizes your certainty. The Attack, landing while you are already unsteady, knocks you off the topic entirely. The Reverse, arriving last, catches you when you are confused and off balance and turns your instinct to be fair into an instinct to apologize. Each move prepares the ground for the next. That is why it feels like going underwater. You are not being hit once. You are being moved through a sequence designed to leave you exactly where Vaelan ended up.

I call this the Structure Beneath the Words. The words of a DARVO exchange are infinitely variable, but the structure beneath them is fixed, and once you learn to listen for the structure instead of getting caught in the words, you can track the reversal even while it is happening to you.

When the loop repeats

The three moves do not always run once and stop. In a longer confrontation they often loop. You steady yourself, restate your point, and the sequence begins again from the top: a fresh denial, a new attack, another reversal. This looping is not a sign that you are failing to get through. It is a sign that the sequence is doing its job, which is to wear you down until you give up the original issue simply to end the exchange.

Recognizing the loop protects you from a specific trap, the belief that if you just explain a little better, a little more clearly, one more time, you will reach the person and the reversal will stop. That belief keeps you in the loop, feeding it more chances to work. The structure does not yield to better explanation, because the structure was never about the facts. Once you see the loop for what it is, you gain permission to stop feeding it, which is the seed of the disengagement skill you will build later in this book. For now, simply notice: is this the first pass, or is the tape rewinding to play the same three moves again? Counting the loops is itself a way of staying outside them.

Vaelan's story does not end with a clean victory, and I want to be frank about that because clean victories are rare and promising them would be its own kind of lie. The next time it happened, he still apologized. But he apologized while thinking, clearly and privately, that was the three moves, and he wrote down what the account actually showed before he went to bed. He did not win the conversation. He kept his grip on reality, which at that stage was the win that mattered, and it was the thing that made every later skill in this book possible for him.

What each move sounds like

Because the words change every time, it helps to hold a small bank of examples in your mind, not to memorize but to tune your ear. Here is what each move commonly sounds like across the rooms where you might meet it.

Denial often sounds like: that never happened, you are making this up, I never said that, you are remembering it wrong, I have no idea what you are talking about, that is not how it went. Notice the shared quality, a flat totality that leaves no room for a shared version of events.

Attack often sounds like: you are so sensitive, you always do this, everyone thinks you are difficult, you are the one with the problem, after everything I have done for you, you are crazy, why are you attacking me. Notice how each one moves the subject onto your character, your history, or your motives, and away from the deed.

The Reverse often sounds like: I am the one being hurt here, I cannot believe you would treat me this way, I do everything and get nothing but criticism, you have really shown me who you are, I do not know how much more of this I can take. Notice how each one installs the speaker as the victim and, by clear implication, installs you as the offender.

You do not need to match a sentence to this list to know DARVO is happening. The list is a tuning fork, not a checklist. What you are training is the recognition that a given sentence is doing the job of a Deny, an Attack, or a Reverse, whatever exact words it wears.

The tells in your own body

Here is something that will serve you even when the words are too fast to track. Each move tends to produce a specific reaction in you, and your reaction is often quicker to notice than the tactic itself. Learning your own tells gives you a second, faster way in.

The Deny tends to produce the urge to prove. You reach for your phone, you start reciting evidence, you feel a frantic need to establish a fact you were already certain of. When you catch yourself scrambling to prove the obvious, suspect a Deny.

The Attack tends to produce heat and defense. Your face flushes, your voice rises, you start defending your character, explaining that you are not controlling, not sensitive, not difficult. When you notice yourself defending who you are rather than discussing what happened, suspect an Attack.

The Reverse tends to produce guilt and the impulse to comfort. You soften, you apologize, you reach for the tissue box. When you feel yourself rushing to repair the other person's pain in a conversation you began as the injured party, suspect a Reverse. Your body keeps a faithful record of these shifts even when your mind is swamped (van der Kolk, 2014), and you can learn to read it.

Trying it on your own life

Recognition of the structure grows through slow, deliberate practice on real material, so here are three ways to build it this week.

First, take the example you have been carrying since the Introduction and label the three moves in the margin, one at a time, in order. Do not rush to see all three at once. Find the Deny and only the Deny. Then the Attack. Then the Reverse. Naming them separately trains your ear to hear them separately in real time.

Second, for each move you find, write one short sentence naming the job it did to you. For the Deny: this made me doubt what I knew. For the Attack: this made me defend myself instead of the point. For the Reverse: this made me comfort them. Connecting each move to its effect is what lets you catch it by feel later, before you have even finished analyzing the words.

Third, practice the phrase you will use internally when you notice the structure starting. Something plain, like there is the reversal. Say it a few times now, out loud, so it is available to you under pressure. You are not going to say it to them yet. You are going to say it to yourself, which is where recognition lives.

Fourth, spend one day this week simply counting, in any ordinary disagreement you happen to have, whether the three moves appear. Most ordinary disagreements will not contain them, and that is the point of the exercise. You are calibrating, learning the difference between a hard conversation and a reversal, so that when the real structure shows up you feel the contrast sharply rather than seeing the tactic everywhere. Recognition that cannot tell the difference is not recognition. It is a new kind of fog, and you are training your way out of fog, not into a fancier version of it.

The short version

The turn that feels like water is not water. It is three moves with three jobs. Deny closes the door and makes you audit your own memory. Attack changes the subject from what they did to who you are, using the ordinary way criticism sticks against you (Baumeister et al., 2001). Reverse takes the last role, the victim's role, and turns your empathy back on the person who caused the harm (Freyd, 1997). They usually come in that order because each one softens you for the next. Learn to hear the Structure Beneath the Words, and the sequence stops being weather you endure and becomes machinery you can watch. In the next chapter we look at why this machinery works so well on people who are decent, fair, and willing to consider they might be wrong, because understanding that is how you stop blaming yourself for being caught by it.

Chapter 3: Why It Works on Empathetic People

Solenne kept a mental list of her own faults, and she reviewed it often. She was thirty-three, a person friends described as thoughtful, the one who remembered birthdays and noticed when someone went quiet at a party. When her closest friend borrowed a large sum and then went cold about paying it back, Solenne spent two weeks talking herself out of raising it. She did not want to seem money-minded. She kept imagining the friend's side, kept finding reasons the delay might be fair. When she finally asked, gently, whether they could make a plan, the friend's face hardened, and Solenne felt the familiar sequence begin.

What struck her afterward was not that the tactic had worked. It was how perfectly it had used the best parts of her against herself. Her willingness to see the other side became a door the friend walked right through. Her hatred of conflict became the lever that made her apologize. Her deep discomfort with the idea that she might be unfair became the exact button the reversal pressed. Solenne had always believed her empathy was her strength. That night she wondered, miserably, whether it was actually a defect, the thing that kept getting her hurt.

It is not a defect. That is the heart of this chapter, and I want to reach it early because the belief that your goodness is a weakness is one of the most corrosive things DARVO leaves behind. Your empathy is not the problem. The problem is that a specific tactic is engineered to aim your empathy in the wrong direction. Understanding exactly how it does that will not make you less kind. It will make your kindness harder to hijack.

Your empathy is the handle

Think about what the Reverse actually requires in order to work. It requires that you care whether you hurt people. A person with no empathy at all cannot be moved by someone posing as a victim, because they do not feel the pull to comfort. The Reverse only lands on people who have a working conscience, who feel bad at the thought that they might have caused pain. This is the uncomfortable truth at the center of the tactic. It does not work in spite of your good qualities. It works because of them.

I call this the Empathy Handle. Every object that can be picked up has a handle, a place built for a hand to grip, and the DARVO reversal grips you by your empathy. The fairness that makes you a good friend, the conscience that makes you apologize when you are genuinely wrong, the openness that makes you willing to consider you might have misjudged, these are the handles the tactic reaches for. Knowing where your handles are does not mean cutting them off. Nobody should want to be less fair or less caring. It means knowing when someone has their hand on one and is pulling.

The research underneath the fog

This is not only intuition. When researchers studied what DARVO does to the people who experience it, they found that greater exposure to the tactic was associated with more self-blame in the person who did the confronting (Harsey et al., 2017). Separate work looking at observers found that watching someone deploy DARVO shifted perceptions of credibility, tending to make the person using it appear more believable and the target less so (Harsey & Freyd, 2020). Read those two findings together and you have the machinery of Solenne's night laid bare. The tactic increases your self-blame and decreases your credibility, both to yourself and to anyone watching, and it does this reliably enough to show up in studies.

That word reliably matters. If the effect were random, you might reasonably wonder whether you are just unlucky or unusually fragile. It is not random. It is a documented pattern with a measurable pull, which means the confusion you felt is better understood as the tactic's output than as your personal failing. You did not fall for something obvious. You were subjected to something effective.

Why fair-minded people are the easiest targets

Here is a hard irony to sit with. The very traits that make you a trustworthy person are the traits that make DARVO most effective on you. Consider three of them.

The first is your willingness to doubt yourself. A person who never questions their own perception is oddly immune to the Deny, because they simply do not entertain the possibility that they are wrong. You, being reasonable, do entertain it, which is a virtue in almost every other context and a vulnerability here. The Deny exploits your intellectual integrity.

The second is your sense of fairness. You believe there are two sides to most stories, and there usually are. The Attack and the Reverse exploit this by presenting a competing story, the story where they are the wronged one, and your fairness obliges you to weigh it seriously. A less fair person would dismiss it out of hand. You cannot, because weighing other people's experiences is part of who you are.

The third is your dislike of causing harm. This is the big one, the handle the Reverse grips hardest. Because you would genuinely hate to hurt someone, the accusation that you are hurting them produces real distress, and you move to fix it. The kinder you are, the faster you move. This is why the gentlest people are so often the ones most thoroughly caught. Their kindness is not weakness. It is precisely the thing being used.

The apology reflex

There is a specific behavior that gives fair-minded people away, and it is worth naming because you can catch it in yourself. It is the reflexive apology, the sorry that arrives before you have decided anything is your fault. Solenne apologized four times in a conversation about money she was owed. She was not weighing her guilt and concluding she was wrong. The apology came out of her like a flinch, faster than thought.

This reflex usually has roots. Many people who apologize automatically learned, somewhere earlier in life, that smoothing things over kept the peace and that their own needs were safest when kept small. That learning was once protective. In the presence of DARVO it becomes a liability, because the reflex hands the other person exactly what the Reverse is fishing for, a confession of fault from the only person in the room who did nothing wrong. You do not have to eliminate your good manners to fix this. You have to insert a single beat of awareness between the impulse and the word, long enough to ask whether an apology is actually owed. Most of the time, in these specific moments, it is not. Learning to feel the reflex fire without obeying it is one of the quiet turning points in this work, and later chapters give you concrete ways to hold that beat open.

Betrayal makes it harder to see

There is another reason the tactic works so well, and it has to do with who is usually using it. DARVO tends to come from people you are close to and depend on, a partner, a parent, a close friend, a boss. Freyd's broader research describes how betrayal by someone we rely on can produce a kind of blindness, because seeing the betrayal clearly would threaten a relationship we need (Freyd, 1996). Part of you does not want to fully register that this person, whom you love or need, is manipulating you, because registering it fully is frightening and destabilizing. So you reach for the explanation that costs you less in the moment, which is that the problem must be you.

This is not weakness of character. It is the mind protecting an attachment it depends on. But it means that when the reversal comes from someone close, you are working against a built-in reluctance to see it, and that reluctance is one more reason to trust the pattern rather than your in-the-moment read. If a stranger did this to you, you would see it instantly. It is hard precisely because they are not a stranger.

Why the people watching side against you

One of the loneliest parts of Solenne's experience came later, when she mentioned the situation to a mutual friend and watched the friend's sympathy tilt, subtly, toward the person who owed the money. She felt insane. She had been wronged, and somehow she was losing the room.

She was not imagining it, and it was not a verdict on her. The reversal is designed to work on bystanders too. When someone performs the victim role convincingly, observers who did not see the original events tend to absorb the performance, and their sense of who is credible shifts accordingly (Harsey & Freyd, 2020). The people who did not believe you were not necessarily weak or disloyal. They were responding to a tactic built to produce exactly that response in an audience. Their doubt was the intended output of a deliberate sequence, not a measurement of your worth. Holding this distinction is what lets you keep your footing when support seems to drain away, and it is the foundation for the chapter later in this book on handling the public version of the reversal.

Why it gets worse the more you care

Solenne noticed something painful over the months she thought about this. The tactic seemed to work better on her than it did on other people, and she was right, but not for the reason she feared. It was not that she was more foolish. It was that she was more invested. The more you care about a relationship, the more you have riding on the belief that the other person is fundamentally good, and the more that belief costs you to give up. So you pay a different price instead. You absorb the blame, because absorbing the blame lets you keep the relationship intact in your mind.

This is why the same reversal that a casual acquaintance would shrug off can flatten you when it comes from someone central to your life. Your investment is not weakness. It is love, or loyalty, or need, or all three. But it raises the stakes of every reversal, and it explains why the people who are hurt worst by DARVO are often the most devoted, not the least discerning. If you have wondered why you, of all people, kept getting caught, this is a large part of the answer. You cared, and caring gave the tactic more to work with. None of this means the answer is to care less. A life spent guarding against every possible manipulation by refusing to trust anyone is its own kind of loss, and a worse one. The answer is narrower and kinder than that: keep your capacity to care, and add to it the ability to notice when that capacity is being worked. Those two things can live together, and the rest of this book is largely about teaching them to.

Turning the mirror the right way

The lasting damage of DARVO is not really the argument. It is the slow migration of the question. You start out asking, did they do the thing I raised. You end up asking, what is wrong with me that I keep having these conflicts. The Reverse installs that second question, and once installed it runs on its own, long after the conversation is over. This is the self-blame the research describes, hardening from a feeling into a belief (Harsey et al., 2017).

Undoing it begins with a single act of reframing, which is the practice of this chapter. Every time you catch yourself asking what is wrong with me, you deliberately replace it with a different question: which of my good qualities did that tactic just use. That reframe does two things at once. It stops the self-attack, and it correctly relocates the cause of the confusion, from a defect in you to a design in the tactic. You are not turning off the mirror. You are turning it to face the right direction.

Trying it on your own life

Reclaiming this takes deliberate reps, because the self-blaming question has had a long head start. Here are three ways to practice this week.

First, write your own handle list. Name three genuinely good things about you that this tactic tends to use: perhaps your fairness, your dislike of conflict, your habit of assuming the best. Seeing them written down as strengths, not faults, begins to loosen the grip of the belief that your goodness is the problem.

Second, take one memory where you walked away blaming yourself and run the reframe on it in writing. Ask, of that specific memory, which of my good qualities did the tactic use, and answer in a full sentence. Doing this on paper, slowly, builds the reflex you will later use in real time.

Third, when support seems to drain toward the other person, write one sentence you can hold onto: their doubt is the tactic working on an audience, not a measure of the truth. You are not asking anyone to agree with you. You are refusing to let other people's manipulated impressions rewrite your own knowledge of what happened.

Fourth, watch for your apology reflex for one week without trying to stop it. Simply put a small mark somewhere, a tally on a note, each time you catch yourself apologizing before you have decided anything is your fault. Do not judge the count. The goal is only to make the reflex visible, because a reflex you can see is a reflex you can eventually interrupt, and you cannot interrupt what you have never noticed. By the end of the week most people are startled by how often the reflex fires and how rarely an apology was actually owed. That startle is useful. It is the beginning of choice where before there was only habit.

Where this leaves you

Your empathy is not a defect, and the fact that DARVO worked on you is not evidence against your judgment. The tactic grips you by the Empathy Handle, using your fairness, your self-doubt, and your dislike of causing harm, the very traits that make you trustworthy (Harsey et al., 2017). It works especially well when it comes from someone you depend on, because part of the mind resists seeing betrayal by people it needs (Freyd, 1996), and it works on bystanders too, which is why support can seem to drain away for reasons that have nothing to do with the truth (Harsey & Freyd, 2020). The repair begins by turning the mirror the right way, replacing what is wrong with me with which of my good qualities did that tactic use. That reframe protects your kindness while making it far harder to hijack. But it raises a fair and necessary question, one a forthright book cannot dodge: if I am supposed to trust the pattern over my own doubt, how do I know I am not just excusing myself and refusing real accountability. That is the next chapter, and it is the one that keeps everything else truthful.

Chapter 4: Is This DARVO or Am I the Problem

Caelan almost did not read this chapter, and if you are tempted to skip it too, you are exactly the person who most needs it. He was forty-six, and by the time he learned the word DARVO he had a name for everything his ex-wife did during their divorce. Every denial was DARVO. Every complaint about his behavior was DARVO. Every time she said he had hurt her, he heard the Reverse, and he dismissed it. The word had become a key that unlocked every door, and a key that opens every door is not really a key anymore. It is a way of never having to look inside any room.

The trouble came when their counselor, carefully, showed him a pattern in his own texts. He had, in fact, sent messages at midnight, many of them, insisting she respond. He had, in fact, raised his voice in front of the children more than once. These were real, and they had hurt real people, and he had been filing every mention of them under DARVO so he would never have to hold them. He had taken a genuine tool for recognizing manipulation and turned it into a shield against all accountability, which, and this is the uncomfortable part, is not so different from what the tactic itself does.

This chapter is the conscience of the book. Everything else teaches you to see DARVO and respond to it. This chapter teaches you to be sure it is actually there, because a label this powerful can be misused, including by you, against people who are simply telling you something true that you do not want to hear. Getting this right is not a detour from protecting yourself. It is the thing that makes your self-protection trustworthy, to yourself and to everyone watching.

Why this matters more than it seems

There are two ways to get this wrong, and they cost you differently. The first is to miss real DARVO, to talk yourself out of what is happening and stay stuck in self-blame. Most of this book guards against that error, because it is the more common one for the people who tend to read a book like this. But the second error is real too. It is to see DARVO where there is only an ordinary human being disagreeing with you, or worse, telling you an uncomfortable truth about your own behavior. That error turns a tool for clarity into a tool for avoidance.

The second error is quieter and more seductive, because it feels like strength. It feels like finally standing up for yourself. But if you use the DARVO label to dismiss every criticism, you lose the one thing that separates you from the person who actually manipulates: the willingness to be accountable. I call the safeguard against this the Accountability Test, and it is a small set of probing questions you run before you conclude that what you are facing is a reversal rather than a reckoning.

The Accountability Test

The test rests on a single distinction. DARVO is the evasion of accountability. Legitimate confrontation is the request for it. They can look similar for a moment, especially when you are upset, but they point in opposite directions, and a few pointed questions usually reveal which way you are facing.

Ask yourself, first: am I open to the possibility that I am wrong here. Not required to be wrong, just open to it. A person running DARVO is not open to being wrong, by definition. If you notice that you, too, are completely closed, that no evidence could change your mind, that is worth pausing on, because certainty that admits no doubt is a feature of the tactic, not a sign you are its victim.

Ask, second: is the other person raising something specific that I actually did. There is a difference between a person attacking your character to dodge a topic and a person naming a concrete behavior and asking you to account for it. She missed the deadline is a topic. You send me thirty messages at midnight is a behavior. If what you are calling an Attack is actually a specific, checkable claim about something you did, the fair move is to look at the behavior, not to reach for the label.

Ask, third: does the fault always, without exception, land on the other person. In a real DARVO pattern, you will notice over time that you are never at fault for anything, that every conflict resolves into their guilt and your innocence. Real life is almost never that clean. If your account of every conflict makes you spotless, that is not evidence of your innocence. It is a warning sign about your account.

Ask, fourth: what happens if I grant the other person's point for a moment. Try it as an experiment. If granting their point costs you nothing but a moment of discomfort and might actually be true, you may be looking at legitimate feedback. If granting their point would require you to deny something you directly witnessed with your own senses, you may be looking at a Deny. The test is not foolproof, but it sorts most cases.

Both can be true at once

Here is the distinction that rescued Caelan, and it is the most important idea in this chapter. It is possible to be manipulated and to be wrong at the same time. These are not mutually exclusive. His ex-wife may well have used denials and reversals during their divorce. He also genuinely sent those midnight messages. Both things can be true, and holding only one of them was keeping him stuck.

This matters because manipulators exploit all-or-nothing thinking, and so do we when we are defending ourselves. If you believe that admitting any fault means the other person was right about everything, you will refuse to admit any fault, and you will call every criticism DARVO to protect that refusal. But maturity lives in the middle. You can say, clearly, I did that specific thing and I own it, and also, separately, you are denying and reversing when I raise what you did. Owning your part does not concede theirs. In fact, it is the thing that gives you the standing to name theirs credibly.

When you owe an apology

Sometimes the true answer to this chapter's question is that you are, in this instance, the one who caused harm. That is not a failure of the book. It is the book working. When the Accountability Test points at you, the right response is the one you would want from someone who hurt you: a clean apology, without a reversal of your own. Name the specific thing, acknowledge the impact, do not smuggle in an excuse or a counterattack, and change the behavior. A real apology has no but in it.

Learning to do this well is also, quietly, protective. People who can apologize cleanly are much harder to manipulate, because they are not carrying a terror of ever being wrong that a skilled manipulator can press. Self-compassion research suggests that people who can meet their own failures with candor rather than harsh self-attack are actually more able to take responsibility, not less, because they are not fighting to protect a fragile self-image (Neff, 2003). Owning your genuine faults is not the opposite of standing up to DARVO. It is part of the same steadiness.

A quick outside check

When you are too close to a conflict to judge it, borrow an outside view. One simple version is to imagine the same exchange happening to someone you love, described to you exactly as it happened, with the roles kept straight. If your friend told you, I raised that he missed the deadline and he told me I was crazy and impossible and then cried about how hard I make his life, you would probably see the pattern in a heartbeat. We are far clearer about other people's situations than our own, because we are not standing inside the fog with them.

Another version is to write the story twice, once from your point of view and once, from theirs, doing your genuine best to make their case. If their version, written fairly, still requires them to deny things you directly witnessed and to cast themselves as the only victim, the pattern is probably real. If their version, written fairly, turns out to be reasonable and human, you may have been closer to ordinary conflict than to a reversal. This exercise is uncomfortable precisely because it works. It forces you out of the single story that self-protection prefers.

When they call you the manipulator

Here is a turn that catches many readers off guard. Once a word like DARVO enters the culture, manipulators learn it too, and one of the sharpest moves available to them is to accuse you of the very thing you are experiencing. You say, you are denying what happened and attacking me. They say, no, you are the one gaslighting me, you are the real manipulator. Now both of you are using the same vocabulary, and an observer cannot tell from the words alone who is telling the truth.

This is exactly why this chapter exists, and why the Accountability Test matters so much. The vocabulary cannot settle it. Behavior can. The person genuinely willing to be accountable can point to specific things they have owned. The person running the tactic cannot, because owning specifics is the one thing the tactic is built to avoid. When you have done the real work of this chapter, when you can name your own real faults and have apologized for them cleanly, you hold something the manipulator does not: a track record of accountability. That record is your ground when the accusation gets turned around, and it is one more reason that the humbling work of this chapter is not a weakness in your position but the strongest part of it. There is a strange freedom in this. Once you have genuinely looked at your own conduct and owned what was yours, you no longer have to fear the accusation, because you have already faced the question yourself and answered it. The person who dreads being called a manipulator is often the person who has not done that looking. The person who has done it can hear the accusation, consider it fairly one more time, and set it down, because they already know what they did and did not do.

When it is genuinely unclear

Sometimes you will run the test and still not know. The situation is murky, you are too close to it, the other person is both wronging you and being wronged. This is common, and pretending otherwise would be untrue. In these cases, resist the pull to force a verdict. You do not have to decide today whether someone is manipulating you. You can hold the question open, keep observing the pattern over time, and rely on the one thing that clarifies almost everything: repetition. A single confusing conversation could be anything. A pattern that repeats across months, in which your reality is always denied, your character is always attacked, and they are always the victim, is much harder to mistake. Time is a truth-teller. Let it work.

Trying it on your own life

This chapter's practice is uncomfortable on purpose, because truthfulness about yourself is what makes everything else in the book trustworthy.

First, take a current conflict you have been labeling as DARVO and run all four Accountability Test questions on it in writing. Answer plainly, especially the third and fourth. If the label survives a searching test, you can trust it far more. If it does not, you have learned something more valuable than a confirmation.

Second, complete this sentence about the same conflict: the specific thing I may have gotten wrong here is. If you cannot complete it, sit with why. Sometimes the answer is that you truly did nothing wrong, and that is real. Sometimes the inability to find any fault is itself the thing to examine.

Third, if the test points at you on some specific point, draft a clean apology for that point only, with no but, no reversal, and no reference to what they did. Notice how it feels to own one thing without conceding everything. That feeling is the muscle this chapter builds.

Fourth, write the disputed story twice, once in your voice and once in theirs, making their case as fairly and generously as you can. Then read the two versions side by side and notice which one requires denying plain facts and casting a single spotless victim. This takes twenty minutes and a fair amount of nerve, and it is the single most clarifying exercise in this chapter. People are often surprised by what they find, sometimes discovering the pattern is even clearer than they feared, and sometimes discovering that the situation was more mutual and more human than the label allowed. Either discovery is a gain, because either one moves you from a story you are defending to a truth you can actually work with.

Why both errors cost you

It is worth naming what is at stake in getting this right, because the two errors do different damage. Miss real DARVO, and you stay trapped in self-blame, apologizing for harm you did not cause, slowly losing trust in your own mind. See DARVO where it is not, and you become unreachable, unable to hear the ordinary corrections that every relationship requires, and, over time, more like the thing you fear. The people who use this book best are the ones who hold both risks at once, who take the pattern seriously and also stay accountable. That double grip is not a compromise between the two. It is the only position from which either kind of clarity is possible.

The one thing to carry

DARVO is the evasion of accountability. Legitimate confrontation is the request for it. The Accountability Test, four direct questions about your own openness, the specificity of what is being raised, whether you are ever at fault, and what happens when you grant their point, keeps you from turning a tool for clarity into a shield against truth. The core insight is that being manipulated and being wrong can be true at the same time, and holding both is what maturity looks like. When the test points at you, a clean apology with no but in it is not a defeat but a form of strength, and one that makes you harder to manipulate, not easier (Neff, 2003). When it stays unclear, let repetition and time do their slow, patient work. Now that your recognition is anchored in accountability, you can trust it, which means we can turn to a related confusion that trips up almost everyone: how DARVO relates to gaslighting and to plain old defensiveness, and why telling them apart changes how you respond.

Chapter 5: DARVO Gaslighting and Plain Defensiveness

Évren came to the word gaslighting first, the way many people do, and for a while it explained everything. Their manager would say things had been agreed that had never been agreed, would insist Évren had been told about deadlines that no one had mentioned, and Évren, who was thirty and new to the team, started keeping obsessive notes just to hold onto reality. Gaslighting was the word for that, and it fit. But it did not quite cover what happened when Évren pushed back. When they finally said, calmly, that they had a written record showing the deadline was never communicated, the manager did not simply insist again. The manager erupted. Évren was accused of being combative, of building a case, of making the whole team walk on eggshells, and then, within a minute, of being the reason the manager dreaded coming to work.

That eruption was not gaslighting, or not only gaslighting. It was something with more moving parts, and Évren did not have a word precise enough to hold it. This is a common place to get stuck. The self-help vocabulary has grown fast, and terms like gaslighting, DARVO, deflection, and defensiveness get used almost interchangeably, as if they were four names for one thing. They are not. They are different, and the differences are not academic. They change what you should do. This chapter draws the lines clearly, because naming the right thing is the first step to answering it well.

Naming the right thing

There is a reason precision matters here, and it is practical, not pedantic. Each of these patterns calls for a different response. If you treat ordinary defensiveness as if it were a calculated reversal, you will be needlessly cold to someone who was just briefly rattled. If you treat a full DARVO reversal as if it were simple defensiveness, you will keep gently re-explaining yourself into a trap that gentleness cannot fix. I call the skill of matching your response to the actual pattern Naming the Right Thing, and it begins with knowing what each term actually means.

Let us take them one at a time, from the simplest to the most complex, and then look at how they overlap.

Plain defensiveness

Defensiveness is the most ordinary of the four, and the least sinister. It is what almost everyone does when they feel criticized. You raise something, the other person feels attacked, and they push back, make excuses, point out your own faults, get a little heated. It is reflexive and self-protective, and most people, once they calm down, can come back and take responsibility.

The tell of plain defensiveness is that it responds to reassurance and time. If you say, I am not attacking you, I just want to sort this out, and the person visibly settles and re-engages with the actual issue, you were probably dealing with defensiveness. It is a moment, not a strategy. It does not require you to hold your ground against a campaign. It requires ordinary patience, and it usually resolves when both people cool down. Do not reach for the heavy vocabulary of manipulation for something that is just a human being feeling stung.

Deflection

Deflection is a step further. It is the move of changing the subject to avoid accountability, but without the full architecture of a reversal. When you raise a concern and the other person answers by bringing up something unrelated that you did, that is deflection. Well what about the time you forgot my birthday. It dodges, it frustrates, and it can be a component of DARVO, but on its own it does not necessarily deny your reality or cast the other person as the victim. It just refuses to stay on the topic.

Deflection is worth naming separately because the response to it is specific and doable: you name the dodge and return to the point. That is a topic for another conversation. Right now I am asking about this. Deflection often folds once you calmly refuse to chase the new subject, whereas a full reversal will escalate. How the person responds when you decline to be deflected is itself diagnostic. Defensiveness settles, deflection persists mildly, DARVO escalates into attack and reversal.

Gaslighting

Gaslighting is more serious and more specific. It is the sustained effort to make you doubt your own perception, memory, or sanity. The term comes from a play and film in which a husband dims the gas lights in the house and then insists to his wife that they have not changed, methodically making her distrust her own senses. Gaslighting is that, applied to reality itself. You saw what you saw, and someone with more power in the relationship works to convince you that you did not.

What distinguishes gaslighting from an ordinary Deny is its persistence and its aim. A single denial is a move. Gaslighting is a campaign, conducted over time, whose goal is to erode your confidence in your own mind until you rely on the gaslighter to tell you what is real. Researchers who study it emphasize that it usually depends on a power difference and often on the target's genuine trust in the other person, which is what makes it so destabilizing (Sweet, 2019). Gaslighting is frequently present in the Deny stage of DARVO, but it can also occur on its own, as a slow drip rather than a three-part sequence.

Évren's obsessive note-taking was a direct symptom of gaslighting, and it is worth pausing on, because it is one of the clearest signs. When you find yourself documenting ordinary things compulsively, screenshotting conversations, keeping records not for any practical purpose but simply to prove to yourself later that you are not imagining things, that behavior is telling you something. Healthy relationships do not require you to build an evidence file to keep your grip on reality. The need to constantly verify your own memory is often the first clue that someone has been steadily working to make you doubt it. Évren thought the note-taking meant they were paranoid. It meant the opposite. It meant some part of them was fighting, correctly, to hold onto the truth.

How DARVO contains and exceeds them

Now the reason all of this was worth sorting out. DARVO is not a separate item on the same list. It is a larger structure that can contain the others. Its Deny stage often is gaslighting. Its Attack stage often includes deflection. What makes DARVO distinct is that it does not stop there. It adds the third move, the Reverse, in which the person who caused the harm claims the role of victim and hands you the role of offender (Freyd, 1997). That role reversal is the signature that tells you this is DARVO and not merely one of its parts.

Think of it as a matter of completeness. Defensiveness is a flinch. Deflection is a dodge. Gaslighting is an assault on your grip on reality. DARVO is all of these organized toward a single end, escaping accountability by making you the accused. When you can see whether the third move, the Reverse, is present, you can tell the whole structure from its pieces, and that single distinction resolves most of the confusion people carry into this topic.

Why these get confused in the first place

It is worth understanding why the vocabulary collapsed into a single blur for so many people, because understanding it protects you from doing it again. Part of the reason is speed. These terms entered everyday conversation quickly, spread through short videos and posts that rarely have room for careful distinctions, so a great many people learned all four words in the same week from the same sources, with the differences sanded off. Part of the reason is that the patterns genuinely overlap, so any real example tends to contain more than one of them, which makes them feel inseparable. And part of the reason is emotional. When you are hurt, the precise mechanism of the hurt is the last thing on your mind. You just want a word for the pain, and any of the four will do as a container for it.

None of that is a failing. But precision is a tool, and a blurred tool works poorly. The person who can say, this specific thing is gaslighting and this other specific thing is a reversal, is far better equipped than the person for whom it is all just toxic. Toxic is a feeling. The four names are a map, and you can act on a map. And acting on a map beats thrashing in a feeling every single time, because a feeling only tells you that something hurts, while a map tells you where you are and which way to move. That is the practical gift of precision, and it is why this sorting work, which can seem merely tidy, is really about restoring your power to act.

A side by side look

It can help to hold the four next to each other by their defining question and their right response. Defensiveness asks, in effect, why are you attacking me, and settles when it feels safe. Deflection asks, what about your faults, and folds when you decline to chase it. Gaslighting insists, that is not what happened and you know it, over and over, until you doubt yourself, and it calls for outside records and distance. DARVO runs all the way to, I am the real victim here and you are the one hurting me, and it calls for the full set of responses this book is building toward.

Notice that the four form a kind of ladder, each rung containing more than the last. Defensiveness is a feeling. Deflection adds a dodge. Gaslighting adds an assault on your reality. DARVO adds the role reversal on top of all of it. Climbing the ladder in your mind, rung by rung, is often the fastest way to locate exactly where a given conflict sits, and locating it is what tells you which response to reach for.

A simple way to tell them apart

You do not need to run a technical analysis in the moment. You need one question, asked afterward, in order. Did they change the subject to avoid the issue. If no, it may have been simple defensiveness. If yes, ask the next question. Did they work to make me doubt my own memory or perception. If yes, gaslighting is in play. Then the deciding question. Did they end up positioned as the victim, with me cast as the one who wronged them. If yes, you were not dealing with a piece. You were dealing with the whole reversal, which is DARVO.

Évren ran this sequence on the eruption with their manager and found all three. The subject was changed, their record was denied in a way meant to make them doubt it, and the manager ended the exchange as the wounded party dreading work while Évren stood accused of poisoning the team. That was not four possible words for one event. It was DARVO, with gaslighting inside its first move and deflection inside its second, and naming it correctly told Évren something useful: gentle re-explanation, which is the right medicine for defensiveness, was exactly the wrong medicine here, because it would simply feed the loop.

Trying it on your own life

The practice for this chapter is sorting, because sorting is the skill.

First, take three difficult conversations from your past and label each one: defensiveness, deflection, gaslighting, or DARVO. Use the three-question sequence. Some will surprise you. A conflict you filed under DARVO may turn out to have been ordinary defensiveness, and a situation you dismissed as no big deal may reveal the full reversal on closer look.

Second, for whichever pattern you most often face, write down the response it actually calls for, so you stop applying the wrong medicine. Defensiveness calls for patience. Deflection calls for a calm return to the point. Gaslighting calls for external records and, often, distance. DARVO calls for the responses you will learn in the coming chapters. Matching the medicine to the ailment is the whole point of naming.

Third, notice the escalation test in real time this week. When you decline to chase a changed subject, watch what happens. Settling suggests defensiveness. Mild persistence suggests deflection. Escalation into attack and role reversal suggests DARVO. You are using the other person's response to your boundary as a diagnostic, which is a quietly powerful move.

Fourth, build your own one line definitions of the four, in your own words, and keep them somewhere you can find them. The act of writing a definition you actually understand, rather than one you copied, is what makes it available to you under stress. When you can reach for your own plain sentence, this is the one where they end up the victim, you have made the distinction yours.

When one person uses all four

A caution before we leave this. Sorting the patterns does not mean each person you struggle with will only ever use one of them. A single manipulative person may be defensive on Monday, deflect on Tuesday, gaslight across weeks, and run a full reversal when finally cornered. The point of naming is not to assign someone a permanent category. It is to identify which pattern is in the room right now, in this specific exchange, so you can choose the right response for this moment. The same person can require patience in one conversation and firm disengagement in the next. Reading the exchange in front of you, rather than the label you have assigned the person, keeps you responsive to what is actually happening instead of fighting the last battle.

This is also a mercy, in a way, because it leaves room for the possibility that a person who was defensive today is not beyond ordinary repair, while still letting you name a reversal clearly when one arrives. You are not sentencing anyone. You are reading the weather in the room and dressing for it.

The short version

Defensiveness, deflection, gaslighting, and DARVO are not synonyms. Defensiveness is a flinch that settles with patience. Deflection is a dodge that folds when you refuse to chase it. Gaslighting is a sustained campaign to make you doubt your own reality, usually resting on a power difference and your trust (Sweet, 2019). DARVO is the full structure that can contain all three and adds the decisive move, the reversal of victim and offender (Freyd, 1997). Naming the Right Thing matters because each pattern calls for a different response, and the deciding question is always the same: did they end up cast as the victim, with you as the offender. If yes, you know what you are facing, and you can stop applying gentle re-explanation to a problem that gentleness only feeds. With recognition now precise, we can turn to the first response skill, and it is not a clever line. It is learning to steady your own body before you say anything at all.

Chapter 6: Steady Your Body First

Lysant knew exactly what she wanted to say. She had written it down, practiced it, refined it until it was clear and calm and fair. She was twenty-nine and had spent a lifetime being told she was too emotional, so she had prepared this confrontation with her mother like a lawyer preparing a case. And then her mother opened with the denial, and something happened in Lysant's body that no amount of preparation had touched. Her chest went tight. Her face flooded with heat. The careful sentences she had rehearsed evaporated, and what came out instead was a rush of words she did not plan, too loud and too fast, which her mother promptly used as proof that Lysant was, as always, out of control.

Lysant left that conversation convinced she had failed because she was not calm enough, not smart enough, not good enough with words. But the problem was not her words. The problem was that she tried to use her words while her body was in an alarm state, and a body in an alarm state does not have access to careful language. This is the piece almost every book on manipulation skips, and it is the piece that makes all the clever responses in the later chapters actually usable. You cannot execute a skilled response while you are physiologically flooded. So before we teach you what to say, we have to teach you how to be steady enough to say it.

Regulate before you reply

Here is the principle that reorders everything: regulate before you reply. Your nervous system moves faster than your reasoning mind. By the time you consciously think, this is DARVO, your body has often already shifted into a threat state, and that state narrows your options to the ancient ones, fight, flee, freeze, or appease. None of those produce a measured response. Fight makes you explode, which the reversal uses against you. Flee makes you leave without holding your ground. Freeze makes you go blank. Appease makes you apologize. Every one of these hands the tactic what it wants.

This is not a character flaw and it is not something you can fix by trying harder to stay calm. The shift into a threat state is automatic, wired deep, and older than thought (Porges, 2011). You will not out-argue it or out-willpower it. What you can do is learn to work with it, to send your body the specific signals that tell it the emergency is not what it thinks, so that access to your reasoning mind returns. That is a physical skill, not a mental one, and like any physical skill it can be practiced until it is reliable. Think of it the way you might think of learning to brake smoothly in a car. The first time, in an emergency, you stamp and skid. With practice, the motion becomes smooth and nearly automatic, available exactly when the road turns bad. Regulation is the same. What feels impossible in early attempts becomes, with repetition, something your body simply knows how to do, and it will do it for you at the moment you have the least conscious capacity to summon it deliberately. That is the quiet promise of this chapter: the steadiness you cannot find by force now is the steadiness you can build by practice for later.

What flooding actually is

When you perceive a threat, and a personal attack from someone who matters registers as a genuine threat, your body prepares for danger. Stress chemistry rises. Your heart rate climbs. Blood moves toward your large muscles and away from the parts of your brain responsible for nuanced language and careful judgment. This is superb design if you are facing a predator. It is a disaster if you are facing a manipulator, because it strips you of exactly the capacities you need, the capacity to think clearly, to find precise words, to weigh options, to stay on point.

Researchers who study trauma and the body describe how thoroughly this physiological state can override conscious intention (van der Kolk, 2014). This is why Lysant's rehearsed sentences vanished. They were stored in a part of her that the flood had temporarily cut off. Understanding this changes how you treat yourself afterward. You did not fail because you are weak. Your body did precisely what bodies do, and no one thinks their way out of that state by insisting they should be calmer. You get out of it by giving the body different information.

The fastest reset, the long exhale

The single most useful tool is your breath, and specifically the exhale. Here is why it works. Your breathing is connected to the system that governs your alarm state, and the out-breath is linked to the branch of that system that calms you down. When you make your exhale longer than your inhale, you are physically nudging your body toward its settling response (Porges, 2011). This is not a metaphor or a nice idea. It is a lever you can pull on your own physiology, and it works in under a minute.

The method is simple enough to use in the middle of a conversation without anyone noticing. Breathe in for a slow count of four. Breathe out for a slower count of six, or eight if you can. Repeat this three or four times. The longer out-breath is the active ingredient, so do not rush it. You are not trying to fill your lungs. You are trying to lengthen the release. Practiced a few times in calm moments, this becomes available to you under pressure, which is the whole point, because a tool you have never used when calm will not appear when you are flooded.

Grounding when breath is not enough

Sometimes the flood is strong enough that breath alone does not fully clear it, and you need to bring your attention forcibly back into the present, out of the spinning thoughts and into the room. This is grounding, and it works by giving your senses something concrete to hold. Press your feet into the floor and notice the pressure. Name five things you can see. Feel the texture of the chair, the temperature of the air, the weight of your own hands. These small acts pull your attention out of the threat narrative your mind is spinning and back into physical reality, where, in this moment, you are actually safe.

Grounding matters because DARVO works partly by generating internal chaos, a swirl of self-doubt and half-formed defenses and rising panic. Anchoring your attention in your senses interrupts the swirl. You cannot stop the other person from running the tactic, but you can refuse to let it carry your mind away, and a mind that stays in the room is a mind that can still choose its next move.

The strategic pause

Here is the response that Lysant eventually built her recovery around, and it is deceptively powerful. You do not have to respond in the moment at all. The belief that you must answer right now, while the reversal is fresh and your body is flooded, is one of the quiet ways these conversations trap you. You are allowed to pause. You are allowed to say, I need a minute, and step away. You are allowed to say, I am not going to get into this right now, and continue it later, when you are regulated and clear.

Stepping away is not losing. This is worth repeating, because everything in a flooded state screams that leaving means defeat. It does not. Disengaging to regulate is a deliberate, strategic act that protects your ability to respond well. The conversation does not have a scoreboard that resets if you leave. What is actually happening when you pause is that you are declining to hand the tactic a version of you that is too flooded to think. You will come back with your reasoning mind restored, which is a far stronger position than staying and unraveling. Lysant's turning point was the day she learned to say, I need to think about this, and walk to another room, and breathe, before she said anything else.

The appease response deserves special attention

Of the four automatic states, one deserves particular attention because it is the one that most often goes unrecognized, and it is the one the reversal is built to trigger. It is appease, sometimes called fawn. Fight and flight are obvious, and freeze feels unmistakable, but appease can masquerade as being reasonable. You feel the flood, and instead of exploding or leaving, you become accommodating. You soften your tone, you concede points you do not actually believe, you apologize, you rush to smooth everything over. It can look, from the outside and even from the inside, like maturity. It is often panic wearing the mask of politeness.

Appease is worth naming because it is invisible to the person doing it. Lysant could tell when she exploded, because the aftermath was loud. She could not always tell when she appeased, because appeasing felt like keeping the peace, like being the bigger person. But an apology that comes from a flooded nervous system, offered simply to make the threat stop, is not a considered moral act. It is a survival reflex, and the reversal feeds on it. If you learn only one thing about your own alarm states, learn to recognize your appease response, because it is the one most likely to hand the tactic a confession while feeling like grace.

Steadying yourself after it is over

Regulation is not only for the moment of confrontation. Much of DARVO's damage happens afterward, in the replay, when your body stays activated for hours and your mind loops through the exchange, and that prolonged activation is its own kind of harm (van der Kolk, 2014). Learning to bring yourself down after the conversation matters as much as steadying yourself during it.

The same tools work. The long exhale, repeated for a few minutes, tells your body the emergency has passed. Physical movement helps discharge the stress chemistry that the confrontation dumped into you, so a walk is not avoidance, it is regulation. Grounding brings you out of the replay and back into the present. What you are doing, in all of these, is refusing to let the conversation keep running in your body long after it has ended in the room. The person is gone. The threat is over. Your nervous system does not know that yet, and these practices are how you tell it.

When you cannot simply leave

The strategic pause assumes you can step away, and sometimes you cannot. You are in a car, in a meeting, in front of the children, in a situation where walking out is not available. In those moments, the internal tools become your pause. You cannot leave the room, but you can take three long exhales while the other person is still talking. You can ground your feet into the floor and name to yourself, silently, five things you can see. You can create an internal step-back even when an external one is impossible.

You can also buy time with words alone, without leaving. Let me think about that for a moment is a complete sentence, and the pause it creates gives your body a few seconds to begin settling. Silence itself is a tool. You are not obligated to fill it, and a few slow breaths of quiet, however uncomfortable, is often enough to keep you from being swept into the automatic response the moment is pulling for. The goal is always the same, whether you can leave or not: put even a small gap between the flood and your response, because everything good happens in that gap.

Trying it on your own life

This chapter's practice is physical, and it must be practiced when calm so it is available when it is not.

First, learn the long exhale now, before you need it. Breathe in for four, out for six or eight, three times. Do this once a day for a week, in a calm moment, so your body learns the pattern and can find it under stress. This is the most important single practice in the book, because it is the gateway to every response that follows.

Second, choose your pause sentence in advance and say it out loud a few times. Something plain: I need a minute. Let me think about this and come back to you. I am not going to get into this right now. Having the sentence ready means you do not have to compose it while flooded, which is precisely when composing anything is hardest.

Third, practice one grounding technique until it is familiar. Feet on the floor, five things you can see, whatever works for you. Run it a few times this week in ordinary moments, so that in a hard moment your attention has a trained path back into the room.

Fourth, after your next hard conversation with this person, do not go straight back to your day. Take ten minutes to bring yourself down deliberately: a short walk, a few minutes of long exhales, a grounding round. Notice how long your body stays activated when you do nothing, and how much faster it settles when you help it. Learning your own recovery time is useful information, because it tells you how much space to leave yourself after these encounters, and it teaches your body that the storm always passes, which, over time, makes the storms themselves a little smaller.

A last word on self-treatment, because it matters. If you have exploded, gone blank, fled, or appeased in the past, and you almost certainly have, none of that was failure. It was a nervous system doing its oldest job under fire. The reason to build these skills is not that your reactions were shameful. It is that you deserve to have access to your own clear mind in the moments you most need it, and that access is trainable. You are not fixing something broken in you. You are giving something good in you a fighting chance to show up.

What to carry forward

You cannot use a skilled response while your body is in an alarm state, and that state is automatic, not a weakness (Porges, 2011). The reversal pushes you toward fight, flight, freeze, or appease, and every one of those hands the tactic what it wants. So the first response skill is not a clever line. It is to regulate before you reply, using the long exhale to nudge your body toward calm, grounding to pull your attention back into the room, and the strategic pause to buy the time your reasoning mind needs to come back online. Stepping away to steady yourself is not defeat. It is the move that makes every other move possible. With your body steadier, you are finally ready for the words, and the next chapter gives you the six responses that actually work once you are calm enough to use them.

Chapter 7: Six Responses That Hold

Auren had read enough by now to recognize the tactic, and he could even keep his body reasonably steady during it, which was more than he could once have said. What he still did not have was any idea what to actually do. He was fifty-two, and he had spent a long marriage learning to smooth things over, so when his adult son ran the familiar sequence during a disagreement about a family loan, Auren recognized every move as it happened and still felt helpless. He could name the Deny, feel the Attack, see the Reverse, and yet he stood there with nothing to say, because recognition without response is only a clearer view of the trap.

That is the gap this chapter closes. Recognizing DARVO and staying calm are necessary, but they are not enough on their own. You need a small set of responses you can actually reach for, ones that hold your ground without escalating, that keep you out of the loop rather than feeding it. There are six of them. None is a magic phrase that stops a manipulator, because no such phrase exists, and any book promising one is selling something. What these six do is keep you standing on your own ground, which, it turns out, is the only victory available and also the only one you need.

Hold the ground

Everything in this chapter serves one principle, which I call Hold the Ground. In a DARVO exchange, there is your ground, the original issue and your own reality, and there is their ground, a shifting territory of denials, attacks, and role reversals designed to pull you off your footing. Almost every mistake people make in these conversations is a version of the same mistake: they step onto the other person's ground to argue there. They defend their character against the Attack. They try to disprove the Reverse. They re-litigate the Deny. Each of these steps, however reasonable it feels, abandons the only ground you can actually hold.

To hold the ground means to stay with your issue and your reality, and to decline, gently and repeatedly, every invitation to fight somewhere else. The six responses are six ways of doing that. Read them not as a script to recite in order but as a set of tools, any one of which might be the right one for a given moment.

Response one, name it internally

The first response happens entirely inside you, and it is the foundation for all the others. The moment you sense the sequence beginning, name it to yourself. This is DARVO. There is the Deny. Now the Attack. Here comes the Reverse. This internal naming is not decoration. It is what keeps you in the observer position rather than the swept-along one, and it is supported by the same logic that runs through this whole book, that understanding the tactic reduces its power over you (Harsey & Freyd, 2020). Naming internally also creates a small, crucial distance between what is happening and your reaction to it, and in that distance you can choose. Every other response depends on this one, because you cannot deploy any tool while you are lost inside the confusion the tactic is manufacturing.

Response two, do not defend the reversal

The second response is a discipline of restraint, and it is the hardest for most people. When the reversal casts you as the villain, every instinct says to defend yourself, to prove you are not controlling, not abusive, not the problem. Do not. The instant you begin defending against the reversal, you have stepped onto their ground and the tactic has succeeded, because the conversation is now about your character instead of their behavior. Defending the reversal is the trap, not the escape.

This does not mean you accept the accusation. It means you decline to argue it. There is a difference between defending, which engages the accusation on its terms, and declining, which sets it aside. I am not going to defend myself against that is a complete and powerful response. It refuses the bait without conceding the point, and it keeps you standing where you began. Auren's breakthrough came when he realized that his long, careful explanations of why he was not the bad guy were not clearing his name. They were proof, to his son, that the reversal had landed, because only a person who feels accused explains so hard.

Response three, restate the issue once

The third response is the positive counterpart to the second. Having declined to fight on their ground, you calmly return to yours by restating the original issue, once. Not repeatedly, not with mounting emphasis, not as if volume or repetition will finally make it land. Once, plainly. What I raised is that the loan was not repaid, and that is what I want to talk about. Then you stop.

The word once matters, because repetition pulls you into the loop. If you restate the issue five times, each time louder, you are no longer holding the ground, you are pacing frantically on it, and that frantic pacing is exactly what the reversal wants to provoke, because it makes you look unhinged. Say it once, cleanly, and let the silence sit. You are not required to make the other person agree, engage, or even acknowledge. You are only required to keep your own footing, and one calm restatement does that far better than ten heated ones.

Response four, refuse the role reversal

The fourth response directly addresses the heart of the tactic. When the person installs themselves as the victim and you as the offender, you decline the assigned role. You do not have to justify why you spoke up. You do not have to accept the part you have been handed.

I am not the one who did something wrong here, and I am not going to act as if I am, is a clean refusal of the reversal.

This is different from defending against the reversal, and the distinction is subtle but important. Defending argues the case, which keeps you on their ground. Refusing simply declines to accept the framing, which keeps you on yours. It is the difference between saying, let me explain all the reasons I am not controlling, which engages the frame, and saying, I am not going to accept being cast as the villain for raising a real concern, which rejects the frame outright. You are not debating your innocence. You are refusing to enter a trial you never should have been put on.

Response five, disengage

The fifth response is the one people most need permission to use, so let me give it plainly. You can leave. DARVO feeds on prolonged interaction, on the loop that keeps running as long as you keep engaging, and one of the most effective things you can do is stop feeding it. I have said what I needed to say. I am going to step away now. Then you go.

Disengaging is not conceding. It is refusing to participate in a process designed to wear you down. There is rarely anything to be won by staying in a reversal past the point where it is clear the person will not engage, and there is much to be lost, because the longer you stay, the more chances the tactic has to catch you. Walking away with your reality and your dignity intact is a win, even though the flooded, fight-oriented part of you will insist it is a surrender. It is not. It is often the wisest move available, and the strongest.

Response six, bring a witness

The sixth response changes the conditions rather than the words. DARVO is significantly harder to run in front of a witness who understands the tactic, because the reversal depends on there being no one present to see the sequence clearly. When you can, do not have the highest-stakes conversations alone. Bring a trusted friend, a family member, a colleague, someone who knows what to look for. Their presence does not guarantee good behavior, but it raises the cost of the tactic and gives you an external anchor for reality, someone who saw what you saw.

For conversations you cannot have with a witness physically present, a written channel can serve a similar function, because it creates a record that a third party could later read. The point in both cases is the same, to remove the privacy that the reversal relies on. A tactic built on there being no witnesses works far less well when a witness is there.

There is a reason this response is placed last, and it is not that it matters least. It is that arranging a witness takes forethought, which the earlier responses do not. The first five you can reach for in any moment. The sixth you build in advance, by choosing not to walk into a predictable reversal alone, by moving an important conversation to a place or a format where someone else can see it. When you know a hard exchange is coming, and often you do, the single most protective decision you can make is made before the conversation starts, in the quiet choice of where, how, and with whom it will happen. That decision is yours to make, and making it well can do more for you than any line you could deliver once the reversal is already underway.

What these responses are not

It is worth being clear about what these six responses will and will not do, because false expectations are how people conclude the tools do not work and give up on them. These responses will not make the other person see reason. They will not produce an apology, an acknowledgment, or a moment of insight in which the manipulator suddenly understands what they did. If you use them hoping for that, you will be disappointed every time, because a person committed to the reversal is not available for that kind of resolution, at least not in the heat of it.

What these responses will do is protect you. They keep you from being pulled off your ground, from confessing to things you did not do, from unraveling in a way that gets used against you, from staying in a draining loop long past the point of any use. The shift you have to make, and it is a genuine shift, is from measuring success by their response to measuring it by yours. Did I keep my footing. Did I decline the assigned role. Did I leave when leaving was right. Those are the questions that determine whether you succeeded, and every one of them is about you, which means every one of them is within your power. That relocation of the scoreboard, from their behavior to your own, is quietly one of the most freeing moves in this entire book.

How they fit together

Although you will not run all six like a checklist, they do have a natural flow, and it helps to see it. Naming internally comes first and runs underneath everything, the steady inner voice tracking the pattern. From that observer stance, you decline to defend the reversal and instead restate your issue once, holding your ground positively. If the person accepts the role reversal frame anyway, you refuse the role without arguing it. If the loop simply repeats, you disengage. And where the stakes are high enough, you arrange from the start to have a witness present, so that the whole exchange happens in conditions less friendly to the tactic.

You might use only one of them in a given moment. A brief reversal from a friend might need nothing more than an internal naming and a single calm restatement. A grinding, high-stakes confrontation with someone who will not stop might require all of them, ending in disengagement. Reading which tools a given moment needs is a skill that grows with use, and early on it is perfectly fine to lean on just the two you have rehearsed. You are not being graded on elegance. You are keeping your footing, and any tool that does that is the right one.

Trying it on your own life

You will not use all six at once, and you should not try. The practice is to make a few of them yours.

First, choose the two responses you will reach for first, based on the person and situation you most often face. Write them on a card or a note on your phone, in your own words. Having two ready is far more useful than vaguely knowing all six.

Second, rehearse them out loud, alone, until they sound like you. A response you have said aloud in a calm room is one you can find in a hard one. Say your restatement, your refusal, your disengagement sentence, several times, until they stop feeling like lines from a book and start feeling like things you would actually say.

Third, before your next likely encounter, decide in advance what your disengagement point is. Name to yourself the moment at which you will step away: when the loop repeats twice, when the attack turns to your character, whenever you choose. Deciding in advance means you are not trying to make that call while flooded, and it makes leaving something you planned rather than something you failed to prevent.

Fourth, after your next encounter, grade yourself on the right scoreboard. Do not ask whether the other person changed, apologized, or backed down, because those were never yours to control. Ask instead: did I keep my footing, did I decline to defend the reversal, did I restate my issue without spiraling, did I leave when I had planned to. Write down one thing you did well and one thing you want to do differently next time. Measuring yourself this way, rather than by their reaction, is how you will actually see your own progress, which in the early going is often invisible if you are only watching them. You are getting better at this even on the days the other person does not budge an inch, and this practice is how you prove that to yourself.

Putting it together

Recognition and calm are not enough on their own, and the gap between them and action is closed by six responses that all serve one principle, Hold the Ground. Name it internally, so you stay the observer. Do not defend the reversal, because defending steps onto their ground. Restate the issue once, cleanly, then let it sit. Refuse the assigned role of offender without arguing the case. Disengage, because the tactic feeds on the loop and leaving starves it. Bring a witness, because the reversal relies on privacy. None of these stops a determined manipulator, and none is meant to, because the goal is not to control them. The goal is to keep your own footing, your own reality, and your own dignity, and these six responses do exactly that (Harsey & Freyd, 2020). What they do not yet give you is the exact words for the hardest moments, and that is the next chapter, where the six responses become specific, ready lines you can carry into the room.

Chapter 8: Scripts for the Reversal

Noélin used to freeze at exactly the wrong moment. She was thirty-five, quick-witted in every part of her life except this one, and when her partner ran the reversal she would find her mind gone completely blank, the way a stage actor's might if the lines simply vanished. Afterward, in the car or the shower, the perfect responses would arrive in a flood, clear and calm and exactly right, mocking her with their lateness. She did not lack intelligence or courage. She lacked something smaller and more fixable: ready words. In the flooded moment, with her reasoning mind offline, she had nothing pre-loaded to reach for, so she reached for nothing.

This chapter fixes that specific problem. The previous chapter gave you six responses as principles. This one turns them into actual sentences, the kind you can memorize, adapt, and have waiting when your mind goes blank. Think of these as a starting set, not a rulebook. The goal is not to recite them exactly. It is to have said something like them so many times, in calm moments, that a version of them is there for you when you need it. A line you have rehearsed is a line you can find with your reasoning mind switched off, and that availability is the entire point.

Lines that do not bend

The principle here is what I call Lines That Do Not Bend. A good response to the reversal has a particular quality: it holds firm without escalating. It does not plead, it does not attack, it does not over-explain, and it does not leave a handle for the tactic to grab. It simply states your position and stops. The best of these lines are short, because short lines are easier to remember under pressure and harder to twist. The longer and more elaborate your response, the more surface area you give the reversal to work with. Brevity is not just easier. It is safer.

We will move through the lines by the situation that calls for them, so you can find the right one fast. For each, the aim is the same, to keep you on your own ground.

When you need to hold your point

These are the lines for restating your issue without being dragged off it. What I raised is the thing I want to talk about, and that has not changed. I hear that you see it differently, and the concern I brought is still the concern I brought. We can come back to that, but right now I am talking about this. Notice the shape of these. They acknowledge nothing false, they concede no ground, and they return, calmly, to the point. They do not argue that you are right. They simply refuse to abandon your subject, which is a different and stronger move than winning the argument.

The tone that carries these matters as much as the words. Said with heat, they become fuel. Said flatly, almost boringly, they are difficult to twist into evidence of your instability, because there is nothing dramatic in them to reflect back at you. Aim for the tone you would use to state a simple fact about the weather. Level, unhurried, done.

When you need to decline the fight

These are the lines for refusing to defend against the Attack and the Reverse. I am not going to defend myself against that. I am not going to argue about my character right now. That is not something I am going to get into. Each of these declines the invitation without engaging it. They are complete sentences that end the sub-argument the tactic is trying to start, and they do it without conceding that the accusation has any merit.

The power in these is the refusal itself. When you defend, you accept the premise that the accusation deserves a defense, and you step onto their ground. When you decline, you leave the premise unaccepted and stay on yours. It feels strange at first not to defend yourself, because defending feels like the natural response to an accusation. But you are not in a court that requires your plea. You are in a manufactured trial you can simply decline to attend.

When you need to reject the role

These are the lines for refusing the part of villain that the Reverse assigns you. I am not the one who caused harm here, and I am not going to act as if I did. I came to you with a real concern, and I am not going to be turned into the bad guy for it. I notice that this has become about me being the problem, and it is not going to. These name the reversal, lightly, and step out of the role. You are not debating your innocence. You are declining the casting.

Naming the move, gently, can be especially effective. Something like, I notice we have gone from what happened to what is wrong with me, and I am not going to follow that. This does two things at once. It refuses the role, and it quietly signals that you can see the tactic, which sometimes, though not always, causes the person to abandon a move that only works in the dark.

When you need to leave

These are the lines for disengaging cleanly. I have said what I needed to say, and I am going to stop here. I am not going to keep going in circles, so I am going to step away. Let us come back to this another time. Each of these ends your participation without drama and without a parting shot. The clean exit matters, because a disengagement wrapped in one last accusation of your own just restarts the loop. You are not storming off. You are calmly declining to continue, which is a different energy entirely and much harder to use against you.

What not to say

It helps to know the lines that hand back control, so you can hear yourself starting them and stop. Anything that begins with a frantic defense of your character feeds the reversal: I am not controlling, I am not crazy, how can you say I do not care. Anything that pleads for them to see your side keeps you on their ground: please just admit it, why can you not see what you did, I just need you to understand. And anything that matches their escalation, insult for insult, gives the tactic exactly the unhinged version of you it wants to display. The general rule is simple. If a sentence is long, heated, defensive, or pleading, it is probably working against you. If it is short, level, and returns you to your ground, it is probably working for you.

There is one more category to avoid, and it is the tempting one: the clever comeback, the perfectly cutting line that finally puts the manipulator in their place. It almost never helps. A cutting remark feels satisfying for a second, and then it becomes the new headline, the thing the reversal points to as proof of your cruelty. See how she speaks to me. The wittier and sharper your remark, the more useful it is to the tactic, because it gives the reversal a genuine grievance to work with where before it had none. Resist the comeback. Your goal is not to win the moment with a line people would applaud. Your goal is to walk out with your ground intact, and boring, level, unmemorable sentences do that far better than brilliant ones.

Adjusting the lines by relationship

The four jobs stay the same across every relationship, but the register shifts, and matching the register keeps the lines usable. With a partner, warmth can coexist with firmness, so a line like, I love you and I am still not going to be turned into the villain for raising this, holds the ground without severing the bond. With a parent, especially one you have deferred to your whole life, the lines may need to be simpler and the tone steadier, because the old pull toward compliance is strong: I hear you, and what I said still stands, is often enough. With a coworker or boss, the lines tilt toward the neutral and the documented: as I noted in my message, the deadline was not communicated, and that is the issue I am raising. With a friend, you can often name the tactic more openly, because the relationship may survive the candor: I feel like we have gone from what happened to what is wrong with me, and I do not want to do that with you.

Notice that the job is identical in every case. You are holding your point, declining the fight, rejecting the role, or leaving cleanly. Only the clothing changes. This is why it is worth learning the four jobs rather than memorizing a fixed script. Once you understand what each line is for, you can dress it for whatever room you are standing in.

The flat tone is half the line

A line's words are only half of what it does. The other half is the tone, and here the counterintuitive truth is that flatter is stronger. Every instinct in a heated moment pushes you toward intensity, toward saying the words with force so they will finally land. But intensity is precisely what the reversal wants, because an intense you is easier to portray as the aggressor. The same words delivered flatly, almost wearily, as if you are stating an obvious and slightly boring fact, are far harder to twist. There is nothing dramatic to reflect back at you.

Practice your lines, then, not just for their words but for their temperature. Aim for the tone of someone reading a train timetable. That is not what happened, and that is not what I am here to discuss, said with a shrug in the voice, does more than the same words shouted. The flatness communicates something the manipulator finds genuinely difficult to work with: that you are not rattled, not hooked, not available for the fight. Auren, from the last chapter, noticed that the calmer and more boring his restatements became, the faster his son's reversals ran out of fuel, because a reversal needs an inflamed opponent, and he had stopped supplying one.

A worked example

Let us watch the lines work together in one exchange, using Noélin. Her partner denies having agreed to a shared plan, then pivots: you always rewrite history to make me look bad, you are impossible. Noélin, instead of defending herself as she once would have, breathes once and says, flatly, I am not going to argue about my character. The plan we agreed on is what I want to talk about. Her partner escalates, now wounded: I cannot believe you are attacking me like this, after everything. Noélin does not comfort, does not apologize, does not prove her innocence. She says, I notice this has turned into me being the problem, and I am not going to go there. That is not what happened, and it is not what I am here for. Her partner tries once more. Noélin, having held her ground and seen the loop begin to repeat, closes it: I have said what I needed to. I am going to stop here, and we can come back to it. Then she leaves the room.

She did not win an apology. She did not change her partner's mind. What she did was move through the whole reversal without stepping onto their ground once, without confessing to anything she did not do, and without unraveling. She came out the other side with her reality intact and her dignity whole, which, as you now know, is the only kind of winning this situation offers. And notice how few words it took. Four short lines, none of them clever, all of them holding.

Making the lines yours

Borrowed words feel stiff in the mouth, so the last and most important step is to translate these into your own voice. Take the lines that fit your situation and rewrite them the way you actually speak. If you would never say I am not going to get into that, but you would say that is not what we are talking about, use yours. The words matter less than the function. What you need is a small handful of sentences, in your own idiom, that perform these jobs: hold the point, decline the fight, reject the role, and leave cleanly. Yours will always serve you better than mine, because yours will actually come out of your mouth.

Trying it on your own life

The practice for this chapter is preparation, because the whole problem it solves is the blankness of the unprepared moment.

First, take one line from each of the four situations and rewrite it in your own words, for the specific person you are dealing with. Four sentences, yours, ready. That is the core deliverable of this chapter.

Second, say your four lines out loud, several times, until they feel natural rather than memorized. Do this somewhere private and unhurried. The point is to move them from the page into your mouth, so they are available when the page is nowhere in sight.

Third, put your four lines somewhere you can reach them fast, a note on your phone, a card in your wallet. Before a conversation you know is coming, read them once. You are pre-loading your responses so that when your reasoning mind goes offline, something steady is already there to reach for.

Fourth, practice the flat tone as deliberately as the words. Say one of your lines three ways: heated, pleading, and flat. Hear the difference. Notice how the flat version gives an opponent nothing to grab, while the heated and pleading versions both hand something over. Then practice the flat version a few more times, until the low, level, almost bored delivery feels available to you. In these conversations, your temperature is a tool, and a cool one serves you far better than a hot one. You are not being cold to be cruel. You are being level so that the tactic finds no heat to feed on.

The short version

The problem is rarely a lack of intelligence or courage. It is the blankness of a flooded moment with no words pre-loaded, and the fix is to prepare Lines That Do Not Bend, short sentences that hold firm without escalating. Have a line ready to hold your point, to decline the fight, to reject the assigned role, and to leave cleanly, and know the pleading and defensive sentences to avoid. Then, crucially, translate them into your own voice, because borrowed words come out stiff and yours come out real. Rehearsed in calm moments and kept where you can find them, these lines become available exactly when you need them most, in the moment your mind would otherwise go blank. Words on their own, though, can be denied later, which is why the next chapter turns to the quiet power of a written record, the thing that protects your reality after the conversation ends.

Chapter 9: The Record That Outlasts the Doubt

Orlian started keeping notes almost by accident. He was forty-four, methodical at work and strangely helpless at home, and after one particularly bad exchange with his brother over the handling of their late mother's estate, he sat in his car and typed out what had just happened, mostly to stop his hands from shaking. He did not think of it as evidence. He thought of it as a way to hold onto his own mind. What he did not expect was what happened three weeks later, when his brother described that same conversation to the rest of the family in a version where Orlian had been aggressive and unreasonable and had said things he had never said. For the first time, Orlian did not spiral into self-doubt. He opened his phone, read his own account written minutes after the event, and knew, with a certainty that nothing could shake, what had actually occurred.

That certainty is the subject of this chapter. It is a strange thing to discover that a few sentences typed into a phone can hold more steadiness than years of knowing your own mind, but that is exactly what Orlian found, and it is what this chapter wants to give you. One of the cruelest features of DARVO is what happens after the confrontation, when the other person rewrites the event, insists you misremember, and slowly erodes your confidence in your own recollection. A written record, made close to the event, is the single most powerful defense against that erosion, because memory is vulnerable and a contemporaneous note is not. This chapter teaches you to build that record simply and sustainably, so that when your reality is challenged later, you have something solid to stand on that is not subject to the fog.

The record outlasts the doubt

The principle is straightforward: the record outlasts the doubt. Doubt is what the tactic manufactures, and doubt is corrosive precisely because it works on memory, which is far more malleable than we like to believe. Your recollection of an event can genuinely shift over time, especially under pressure from someone insisting it happened differently, and this is not a weakness unique to you. It is how human memory works. A note written close to the event, by contrast, does not shift. It sits there, unchanged, saying what you knew when you knew it most clearly. When the later doubt arrives, the record is already waiting, and it outlasts the doubt every time.

This matters even if no one else ever reads it. The first and most important reader of your record is you. When your brother, your partner, or your parent tells you that you are remembering wrong, the note lets you check, privately, and reassure yourself. That private reassurance is often enough to keep you from being pulled back into the fog, and it is available to you whether or not the situation ever becomes public, legal, or contested.

Why memory is the battlefield

To understand why documentation matters so much, it helps to understand why memory is where this battle is fought. When someone you depend on repeatedly denies your reality, part of your mind is caught in a genuine conflict, because trusting your own memory means accepting that someone you love or need is lying to you, and that is painful enough that the mind sometimes prefers to doubt itself instead (Freyd, 1996). Add to this the ordinary fact that memory reconstructs rather than replays, and that stress distorts how events are encoded and recalled (van der Kolk, 2014), and you have a recollection that is, through no fault of yours, genuinely vulnerable to being rewritten.

The manipulator does not need to know any of this science to exploit it. They only need to insist, confidently and repeatedly, that things happened differently, and time and doubt do the rest. A written record interrupts that process at its root. It takes the most vulnerable thing, your memory, and gives it an external anchor that cannot be argued into changing its story. This is why survivors are so often counseled, across therapeutic and advocacy settings, to write things down (Herman, 1992). The record is not paranoia. It is the correction to a known vulnerability.

Before, during, and after

The most useful documentation happens in three phases around a confrontation, and each does a different job. Before a conversation you know is coming, write down what you intend to raise and why, in plain terms. This does two things: it clarifies your own thinking so you are less likely to be knocked off your point, and it records your actual intention, which protects you later against the claim that you came in looking for a fight.

During, if the situation allows, note what is happening in the barest terms, though often you will be too engaged for this and that is fine. After is the essential one. As soon as possible once the conversation ends, while it is fresh, write down what was said, in what order, and what the outcome was. Be specific and factual. Record actual words where you can recall them, the sequence of the exchange, the date, and the time. The sooner you write, the more accurate the record, because memory begins its drift immediately. Orlian's habit of typing it out in the car, minutes after, was not incidental to its power. The closeness to the event was the power. A note written a week later, after the other person has already begun insisting on their version, is worth far less, because by then the drift has started and their account has had time to seep into yours. Write while the memory is still yours alone, before anyone has had a chance to edit it, and the record will hold.

Keep it factual, not editorial

A record serves you best when it stays close to what happened rather than what you concluded about it. Write she said the money was never in the account, not she lied about the money, because the first is an observation and the second is an interpretation. This is not about being fair to the other person for its own sake, though it does not hurt. It is about the record's reliability, to you and to anyone who might one day read it. A factual record is one you can trust completely when you reread it, and one that holds up if it ever needs to. An editorial record, full of your conclusions and feelings, is easier to dismiss and harder to trust, even for you.

You can record your feelings too, and you should, but keep them in their own place, clearly marked as your experience rather than as fact. I felt confused and started doubting myself is true and worth noting, and it belongs in a separate line from the record of what was actually said. Keeping the two apart, the events and your response to them, makes both more useful and keeps the factual spine of the record clean.

When the record must do more

For most readers, the record's job is private, to protect your own grip on reality. But for some situations, co-parenting with a manipulator, a workplace dispute, a matter that may become legal, the record may need to do more, and it is worth knowing this in advance. In contexts of ongoing coercive control, careful documentation of patterns over time is often what allows the pattern to be seen at all, because any single incident can be explained away while a documented sequence cannot (Stark, 2007).

If your situation might ever reach that point, a few habits help. Keep the records somewhere the other person cannot access or delete. Date everything. Favor channels that create their own record, such as written messages over verbal conversations, when you are dealing with someone who reverses reality, because a text thread is a record neither of you can later rewrite. This book cannot give legal advice, and if you are in a situation that may become legal you should speak with a professional. But the underlying habit, documenting patterns factually and contemporaneously, serves you whether the record stays private or ever needs to be shown.

The quiet power of writing it down

There is a benefit to documentation that goes beyond defense, and Orlian discovered it slowly. Writing things down changed how he experienced the events themselves. When he knew he would record a conversation afterward, he found he stayed a little more present during it, a little more able to observe rather than only react, because part of him was already the calm narrator who would later write it up. The act of documenting turned him, gradually, from a person swept along into a person keeping a record, and that shift in stance was itself steadying.

This is worth knowing because it means documentation is not only for the aftermath. The habit of recording, once established, subtly strengthens you in the moment, giving you an observer's distance that is hard to hold otherwise. You are building evidence, yes. You are also building a version of yourself that watches, notes, and stays outside the fog, which is the same version every other chapter in this book has been trying to grow.

When writing it down feels like too much

Some readers feel a resistance to documenting, and it is worth naming, because it usually comes from a good place. Writing things down can feel cold, calculating, even disloyal, as though you are building a case against someone you love rather than simply living alongside them. It can feel like admitting the relationship has become the kind where you need evidence, and that admission is genuinely sad. If you feel that resistance, you are not being paranoid or vindictive. You are grieving something.

But consider what the resistance costs. The alternative to a record is not innocence or trust. It is being at the mercy of someone else's version of events, with nothing to hold onto when your own memory is challenged. Documenting is not an act of aggression. It is an act of self-respect, a way of refusing to let your reality be the only thing in the room without a backup. You can keep a record and still hope the relationship improves. The two are not opposed. The record simply means that whatever happens, you will not lose your grip on what was real, and that is a thing you are allowed to protect without apology.

A record protects the relationship too, sometimes

Here is a point that surprises people. A record does not only protect you against the other person. In some relationships, it can actually reduce conflict, because it removes an entire category of argument, the argument about what was said. When both people know there is a written thread, the endless he-said fights have less room to grow, because the words are simply there. This does not work with everyone, and it will not reform a determined manipulator. But in situations that sit closer to the ordinary end of things, moving important agreements into writing can quietly lower the temperature, because it takes memory, the most contested territory, off the table. You are not only arming yourself. Sometimes you are removing the very ground that repeated conflict grows in.

Trying it on your own life

The practice here is to start small and sustainable, because a documentation habit you abandon protects no one.

First, after your next difficult conversation with this person, write a single factual account as soon as you can: what was said, in what order, the date and time, kept close to the events and separate from your interpretations. One entry. See how it feels to have it.

Second, set up an easy place to keep these records, one the other person cannot see, that you can reach quickly. A dedicated note, a private document, an email to yourself. The easier it is to add to, the more likely you are to keep it, and consistency matters more than elaborateness.

Third, the next time this person tells you that you are remembering something wrong, resist the reflex to doubt yourself, and instead go check your record. Notice what it does to your certainty to have written proof of what you knew when you knew it clearly. That feeling, of standing on something solid instead of sinking into doubt, is what this whole chapter is for.

Fourth, where you can, begin shifting important exchanges with this person into written channels. When a significant agreement or plan is made, follow up with a short message confirming it in writing: just to confirm what we agreed, we said the following. This is not a trick. It is a way of creating a shared record that neither of you can later rewrite, and it does its protective work quietly, without confrontation. If the person objects strongly to putting simple agreements in writing, notice that too, because a reluctance to be held to a plain record is itself a kind of information. Candid people rarely mind being quoted accurately. That single observation has clarified many a murky situation for people who were not sure what they were dealing with. Watch how someone responds to the simple act of putting things in writing, and you will often learn more than a dozen conversations could tell you.

A closing reassurance, because the resistance is real for many people. You are not becoming a suspicious, evidence-hoarding version of yourself by doing this. You are protecting one specific thing, your knowledge of what is real, against one specific tactic that targets exactly that. Outside of these conversations, you can go on trusting the people who have earned it and living without a notebook in your hand. The record is a tool for a particular kind of threat, not a new way of moving through the world, and using it where it is needed does not obligate you to use it everywhere.

What to carry forward

The cruelest part of DARVO often comes after the conversation, when your reality is rewritten and your memory, which is genuinely vulnerable, is turned against you (Freyd, 1996; van der Kolk, 2014). A factual record made close to the event is the correction to that vulnerability, because the record outlasts the doubt. Document before, during, and after, keeping the account factual and separate from your interpretations, and store it somewhere safe and dated. For most readers this protects your own grip on reality, and for some it may one day need to do more, in which case documenting patterns over time is what makes the pattern visible at all (Stark, 2007). Beyond its use as defense, the habit itself steadies you, turning you into the observer who watches rather than only reacts. But there is a version of the reversal that a private record alone cannot answer, the one that goes public, where the other person tells everyone their story first. That is the next chapter.

Chapter 10: When They Recruit an Audience

Éloane felt the ground shift before she understood why. She was forty, and she had finally, after years, set a boundary with a longtime friend who had repeatedly taken advantage of her generosity. The conversation itself went the way these do, denial, attack, reversal, and Éloane held her ground better than she once would have. She thought that was the hard part. Then, over the following weeks, she began to notice a coolness from people in their shared circle. A mutual friend, Maevren, who had known her for a decade, became distant. Invitations thinned. When she finally asked Maevren what was wrong, the answer landed like cold water: I heard how you treated her, and I did not think you were that kind of person.

The reversal had gone public. Her friend had not simply denied and attacked and flipped the roles in private. She had taken that same story to everyone they both knew, casting herself as the wounded party and Éloane as the aggressor, and it had worked. People who had known Éloane for years were revising their picture of her based on a version of events they had never witnessed. This is one of the most painful and least discussed dimensions of DARVO, and this chapter is about surviving it. Few things in this whole experience feel worse than watching people you trusted quietly revise their picture of you based on a story you never got to answer, and few things are more important to understand clearly, because the instincts it triggers are almost all the wrong ones. When the reversal recruits an audience, the tactic stops being a private ordeal and becomes a social one, and it requires a different kind of response.

Answer the room, not the rumor

The principle for this chapter is answer the room, not the rumor, and it runs against your every instinct. When you discover that a false version of you is circulating, the overwhelming urge is to chase it, to go to each person and correct the record, to explain what really happened, to prove the story wrong. This almost never works, and often makes things worse, because frantic defense reads as exactly the instability the reversal claimed. The person who runs from friend to friend insisting they are not the villain looks, to onlookers, remarkably like someone with something to hide.

Answering the room instead means tending to the whole of how you show up over time, rather than trying to stamp out each individual rumor. It means letting your steadiness, your consistency, and your character do the slow work of speaking for you, while you decline to perform the anxious defense the tactic is trying to provoke. This is harder than chasing the rumor, because it asks you to tolerate being misunderstood for a while, which is genuinely painful. But it is the response that actually protects you, and understanding why requires seeing how the public reversal works.

Why bystanders believe it

The first thing to hold onto, when people who should know better seem to turn against you, is that their doubt is often the tactic working on them, not a verdict on you. Research on DARVO found that observers who witness the tactic can have their perceptions shifted by it, tending to view the person deploying it more favorably and the target less so (Harsey & Freyd, 2020). The people who cooled toward Éloane were not necessarily disloyal or foolish. They were responding to a convincing performance of victimhood, exactly as the performance was designed to make them respond.

This reframe matters because the social smear produces a specific and terrible loneliness, the sense that everyone can see you are bad, and that loneliness is itself a weapon. Isolation is often the goal, not merely a side effect, because a person cut off from their support is far easier to control and far less able to resist (Herman, 1992). When you understand that the withdrawal of others is the intended output of the tactic rather than a measurement of your worth, you can meet it with grief rather than collapse, and grief you can survive.

The smear is often the point

It helps to understand that when a manipulator broadcasts their version, they are frequently not just venting. They are extending the reversal into your relationships, recruiting others to carry out the tactic on their behalf. The mutual friends who repeat the story, who deliver the cold shoulder, who take the manipulator's side, become, often without realizing it, instruments of the same reversal, mobbing you on someone else's behalf. This is why the experience feels so overwhelming. You are no longer facing one person running a tactic. You are facing a crowd that has absorbed it.

Recognizing this protects you from a specific despair. When friend after friend seems to turn, it can feel like proof that the manipulator was right about you all along, because surely this many people cannot be wrong. But they are not independently arriving at the same conclusion. They are all downstream of a single, skillfully told story, repeating a version they never witnessed. A hundred people repeating one person's account is still just one person's account. The number feels like evidence. It is not. Hold onto that arithmetic when the crowd feels overwhelming. You are not outnumbered by independent witnesses who all saw your wrongdoing. You are facing the reach of a single story, amplified. The reach is real and it hurts, but it does not multiply the truth of the account even slightly.

The lever underneath, your fear of their story

There is a reason the threat of a smear is so effective even before it happens, and it is worth naming because it silences people. Manipulators often threaten, explicitly or implicitly, to tell others their version, to expose you, to turn people against you. This threat works because it presses on something deep, your fear of lost status, of being disbelieved, of being cast out. That fear can keep you from ever raising a concern in the first place, which is precisely its purpose. The threat of the audience is a leash.

The way out of this begins with a hard acceptance. You cannot control what another person says about you, and you cannot guarantee that everyone will believe the truth. Trying to secure that guarantee is what keeps you on the leash. What you can do is decide that the possibility of being misunderstood by some people is a price you are willing to pay for living, rather than a catastrophe you must prevent at all costs. That decision cuts the leash. It does not make the smear pleasant, but it removes its power to silence you in advance.

Build your support before you need it

The single most protective thing you can do about the social dimension of DARVO is to build genuine support before a crisis, not during one. When Éloane looked back, she realized her most important protection was the handful of people whose knowledge of her was deep enough that no secondhand story could dislodge it. Those people did not waver, because their picture of her was built on years of direct experience, not on a single dramatic account. Isolation is the tactic's aim, and connection is the counter (Herman, 1992).

This means investing, in ordinary times, in relationships of real depth, and it means, when a reversal is unfolding, leaning toward those people rather than withdrawing in shame. The instinct under a smear is to hide, to pull away from everyone because it feels like everyone can see your badness. That instinct serves the tactic. Reaching toward your steady people, even when you feel least worthy of connection, is how you refuse the isolation the reversal is engineering. You do not need to convince everyone. You need a few people who know you in the bone, and you need to keep them close.

How to respond to the ones who ask

Not every response is silence, and there is a measured way to speak to people who come to you directly. When someone raises the other person's version with you, you do not have to launch a frantic defense, and you do not have to pretend nothing happened. A calm, brief, non-defensive account is often enough: that is not what happened, and I am not going to get into a back-and-forth about it, but I am glad to tell you my side if you want to hear it. This holds your dignity, offers the truth without forcing it, and declines the anxious over-explanation that would undermine you.

Notice the restraint. You state that the story is false, you offer your account to those genuinely open to it, and you decline to chase those who are not. Some people will want to hear you, and with them a calm, factual account does more than any amount of passionate defense. Others have already decided, and no evidence will move them, and with those people your energy is wasted. Learning to tell the two apart, and to spend your effort only on the reachable, saves you from the exhausting and futile work of trying to convince everyone.

Why time is on your side

The public reversal has one great weakness, and it is time. A dramatic story, told once, can sweep a room. But a manipulator rarely runs the tactic only on you, and rarely tells only one dramatic story. Over months and years, the pattern tends to repeat with other people, and a person who is always the victim, whose every relationship ends in betrayal by someone who was secretly cruel, eventually becomes visible for what they are. The very consistency of the tactic, which is what makes it effective in any single instance, is what exposes it across time.

This is why the steady response, answering the room rather than the rumor, works when the frantic one does not. In the short term, the smear has the advantage, because it is vivid and you are on the back foot. In the long term, your consistency and their pattern do the arguing for you. The people worth keeping are, in the end, the ones who watch how someone actually behaves over years, not the ones swayed by a single compelling account. Éloane found this slowly. Some relationships did not survive the smear, and that loss was real. But over the following year, as her former friend cycled through the same drama with others, several of the people who had cooled quietly came back, having seen the pattern for themselves. Éloane had not chased a single one of them. She had simply kept being who she was, and let time reveal what her frantic defense never could have.

When you share a world you cannot leave

Sometimes the audience is not a friend group you can afford to lose but a world you are bound to, an extended family, a workplace, a co-parenting arrangement, a community. Here the stakes are higher, because you cannot simply let some relationships fall away, and the smear can do lasting practical damage. The principles still hold, but they must be applied with more care. In these settings, documentation matters more, because a factual record can counter a false narrative where your word alone might not. Choosing a few trusted allies within the shared world matters more, because you need people on the inside who see clearly. And restraint matters more, because in a world you cannot leave, an intemperate reaction has a longer memory and a wider reach.

If the shared world is one with formal structures, a workplace with a human resources function, a court with its own rules of evidence, the calm, documented, pattern-focused approach becomes not just wise but necessary, because those structures respond to records and consistency far more than to emotion. This book cannot substitute for professional guidance in those settings, and where real consequences are at stake you should seek it. But the underlying posture, steady, factual, unfrantic, and anchored by a few clear-eyed allies, is what serves you in any audience you cannot walk away from.

Trying it on your own life

The practice here is to prepare for the social dimension before it arrives, and to respond to it with steadiness rather than frenzy.

First, list three to five people whose knowledge of you is deep enough to withstand a secondhand story. These are your anchors. If the list is short, that is useful information, and the quiet work of deepening a few relationships is worth beginning now, in calm times, before any crisis.

Second, write one sentence you can hold onto when support seems to drain away: their doubt is the tactic working on an audience, not the truth about me. Read it when the loneliness of the smear presses hardest. It will not remove the grief, but it will keep the grief from hardening into the belief that you are what the story says.

Third, decide in advance how you will respond to someone who repeats the other person's version to you. Draft your calm, brief, non-defensive line now, so that if the moment comes you are not composing it through a wave of hurt. Having the response ready is what lets you meet the smear with dignity instead of panic.

Fourth, if you are living through a smear right now, resist the urge to hide, and instead reach toward one of your anchor people this week. Tell them plainly that you are going through something and that their steadiness matters to you. You do not need to litigate the whole story or prove your innocence to them. You only need to let one person who knows you stay close, because the tactic wants you isolated, and the simple act of remaining connected to someone who sees you clearly is a direct refusal of what it is trying to do. Connection, not argument, is the antidote to the loneliness the reversal manufactures.

Where this leaves you

When the reversal recruits an audience, the tactic becomes a social ordeal, and it demands that you answer the room, not the rumor. Bystanders who turn are often responding to a convincing performance rather than reaching independent conclusions, because DARVO shifts observers' perceptions in exactly this way (Harsey & Freyd, 2020), and their withdrawal is frequently the intended result, since isolation makes you easier to control (Herman, 1992). Chasing each rumor reads as instability and rarely works. What protects you is steadiness over time, a few deep relationships built before the crisis, a decision to accept being misunderstood by some rather than stay silent forever, and a calm, brief way of speaking to those genuinely open to the truth. The smear is real and it hurts, but it is one person's story no matter how many mouths repeat it. Having faced the tactic in private, in public, and on the page, we turn next to how the same three moves appear across every arena of life, and how to handle the ones you cannot simply walk away from.

Chapter 11: The Same Shape Everywhere

Sevrin thought DARVO was a thing that happened in their marriage, until the divorce, when it followed them into the courtroom. They were thirty-nine, co-parenting two children with a former spouse who had run the reversal for years at home, and Sevrin had assumed that leaving the marriage would end it. Instead the same three moves reappeared in a new costume: denials that agreements had ever been made, attacks on Sevrin's fitness as a parent, and a steady performance of victimhood before mediators, lawyers, and eventually the children themselves. The setting had changed completely. The shape had not changed at all.

This chapter is about that portability. By now you can recognize the three moves, steady your body, respond, document, and withstand a smear. What remains is to see how the identical structure shows up across every arena of life, from intimate relationships to families to workplaces to courtrooms to public life, and to understand what changes and what does not as the setting shifts. The most important practical question this raises is the one Sevrin faced: what do you do when the arena is one you cannot leave, when co-parenting, family, or a job means the reversal is a permanent feature of your landscape rather than a relationship you can end.

Same shape, different stakes

The principle here is same shape, different stakes. The three moves, deny, attack, reverse victim and offender, are constant across every setting, because they are not really about the relationship. They are about escaping accountability, and the structure of escaping accountability is the same whether the person dodging it is a partner, a parent, a colleague, or a public figure (Freyd, 1997). What changes from one arena to the next is not the tactic but the stakes, the tools available to you, and whether you can leave.

This is genuinely good news, because it means every skill you have built transfers. You do not need a new method for each arena. You need the same core skills, calibrated to the setting. Recognizing this saves you from the exhausting belief that workplace manipulation, family manipulation, and co-parenting manipulation are three different problems requiring three different solutions. They are one problem wearing three uniforms. Once you truly absorb that, a great deal of unnecessary overwhelm falls away, because you stop trying to become an expert in several separate fields and start trusting a single set of skills you already have.

DARVO between partners

In intimate relationships, DARVO does its most intimate damage, because the person running it knows you best and the stakes are your closest attachment. Here the reversal often draws on deep knowledge of your insecurities, and the isolation it can produce is total, since a partner can slowly cut you off from other sources of reality. The skills apply directly: recognize the moves, regulate, hold your ground, document, and preserve outside connection. What makes the intimate arena distinct is the depth of the betrayal and the difficulty of seeing clearly someone you love and depend on, which is exactly the betrayal blindness discussed earlier. If leaving is possible and the pattern is entrenched, the intimate arena is often where leaving eventually becomes the answer, though that is a decision only you can make and often not alone.

DARVO from parents

When the reversal comes from a parent, it usually has roots that reach back into childhood, and it carries the extra weight of a lifetime of conditioning. Aeris, a woman in her thirties, discovered that the tactic she was learning to name in her present had been shaping her since she was small. Growing up with a parent who denied her reality, attacked her when she objected, and cast themselves as the wounded party had taught her to accept blame automatically, to distrust her own perceptions, and to soothe others at her own expense. Recognizing DARVO in a parent is often the moment an adult child understands that the self-doubt they have carried their whole life was installed, not innate. The skills apply, but the work is heavier, because you are undoing decades, and this arena has an entire book of its own waiting for those who need to go deeper into it.

DARVO at work

In the workplace, the reversal wears a professional face. A manager or colleague denies commitments, attacks your competence or your character, and positions themselves as the reasonable party burdened by your difficulty. Here the arena provides both constraints and tools. You usually cannot simply leave, at least not immediately, and there may be formal power imbalances that make direct confrontation risky. But the workplace also offers documentation, written communication, and sometimes formal structures that respond to records and patterns. When manipulation is embedded in an institution that fails to address it, the harm compounds, because the institution's failure to respond is itself a form of betrayal (Smith & Freyd, 2014). The workplace arena, too, is deep enough to deserve its own dedicated treatment.

DARVO in court and co-parenting

Sevrin's arena, the family court and the co-parenting relationship, is one of the hardest, because you cannot leave, the stakes involve your children, and the tactic can be weaponized through legal processes. Denials of agreements, attacks on your parenting, and a performance of victimhood before professionals who did not witness the marriage can do real, lasting damage. In this arena, documentation moves from helpful to essential, because a factual record of patterns is often the only thing that can counter a false narrative in a setting built on competing accounts (Stark, 2007). The calm, unfrantic posture matters enormously, because mediators and courts tend to be influenced by who appears stable. This arena, too, has its own dedicated guide, because the specific tools of documentation and process are extensive enough to fill one.

DARVO in public life

The same three moves appear on the largest stages, in politics, in public scandals, in the accounts powerful people give when confronted with wrongdoing. A public figure denies the allegation, attacks the credibility and motives of the accuser, and reframes themselves as the true victim of a witch hunt. Freyd and her colleagues have noted how DARVO operates at this scale, shaping public perception and contributing to confusion about what is true (Harsey & Freyd, 2020). Seeing the tactic in public life is useful for two reasons. It confirms that the pattern is real and structural, not something you imagined in your private life, and it lets you practice recognition at a safe distance, on situations where you have no personal stake and can see the moves clearly.

When you cannot leave

The hardest version of every arena is the one you cannot exit, and it deserves its own principle within the principle. When leaving is not an option, whether because of children, family bonds, financial reality, or professional necessity, the strategy shifts from resolution to management. You stop trying to fix the person or win the relationship, because neither is available, and you focus instead on protecting yourself and, where relevant, those in your care, over the long term.

Management looks like this. You minimize unnecessary contact and keep necessary contact as structured and documented as possible. You favor written channels. You keep your responses brief, factual, and unemotional, giving the tactic as little to work with as you can. You build and protect your support and your outside sources of reality with particular care, because the inability to leave makes isolation more dangerous. And you accept, which is its own kind of grief, that this relationship will not become what you might have hoped, so that your energy goes toward durable self-protection rather than toward a resolution that is not coming. This acceptance is not defeat. It is the redirection of your effort from an impossible goal to an achievable one.

A word on the brief, unemotional response, because it is a specific skill worth naming. When you must keep contact with someone who runs the reversal, giving them flat, factual, minimal communication starves the tactic of fuel. The reversal needs an emotional reaction to work with, a defense to twist, a hurt to exploit. When your responses are short and free of feeling, confirmed for pickup at five, or as noted, the invoice was sent Monday, there is almost nothing for the tactic to grip. This is not coldness for its own sake, and it is not a way of punishing the other person. It is a way of protecting yourself in a relationship you cannot leave, by declining to supply the emotional raw material the reversal runs on. It can feel unnatural at first, especially if you are someone who communicates warmly by default. With practice it becomes a kind of shelter.

When there are children in the middle

The co-parenting arena carries a weight the others do not, because the reversal can reach the children. A co-parent running DARVO may deny things in front of them, cast you as the villain to them, or position themselves as the wounded parent. This is genuinely painful, and it raises the stakes of every skill in this book. Here the goal shifts again, from protecting only yourself to protecting your children's grip on reality without dragging them into an adult conflict.

The core move is to be, for your children, the steady and consistent parent who does not run the tactic, who does not counter-smear, who does not force them to choose. Children are watching who is calm, who is reliable, who does not make them a weapon. Over years, that steadiness registers, even when a dramatic account temporarily sways them, in much the same way that time exposes the pattern to any audience. You cannot control what the other parent says. You can be the parent whose consistency, over the long run, becomes the thing your children trust. This is a marathon, not a single conversation, and it is one of the places where the dedicated co-parenting guide in this series goes far deeper than a single chapter can.

Why practicing on public examples helps

There is a practical reason to pay attention to DARVO in public life, beyond confirming that the pattern is real. Public examples are a training ground with no personal cost. When you watch a public figure deny an accusation, attack the accuser, and reframe themselves as the victim, you can see the three moves with a clarity that is almost impossible when you are the target, because you have no wound in the fight. Studying the tactic where you are only an observer sharpens the eye you will later need where you are the one being reversed.

Use this deliberately. When you notice the pattern in a public story, name the moves to yourself as practice: there is the denial, there is the attack on the accuser, there is the reframe. The reps you build on situations that cannot hurt you transfer directly to the situations that can, and they come without the fog that your own stakes create.

Public life, for all its noise, is a low-cost gym for the recognition skill this whole book depends on.

Trying it on your own life

The practice here is to locate your own primary arena and calibrate your skills to it.

First, name the arena where you most often face the reversal, and write down which of the constraints and tools of that arena apply to you: Can you leave. Do you have documentation available. Are there formal structures. Is there a power imbalance. Knowing the terrain tells you which skills to lean on.

Second, if your arena is one you cannot leave, write a single sentence that marks the shift from resolution to management: I am no longer trying to fix this relationship, I am protecting myself within it. Sitting with that sentence, and the grief in it, is part of the work, and it frees your energy for what can actually be done.

Third, if your situation falls into one of the arenas with its own dedicated guide, co-parenting and family court, the workplace, a narcissistic parent, or being wrongly cast as the abuser, note that a deeper set of tools exists for exactly your terrain, and consider seeking it out when you are ready.

Fourth, practice recognition this week on a public example, where you have nothing at stake. Find a news story or a well-known dispute in which someone confronted with wrongdoing denies it, attacks the accuser, and claims to be the real victim, and name the three moves to yourself as you read. Notice how much easier the moves are to see when you have no wound in the fight. Then carry that clarity back to your own situation, where the fog is thicker but the shape is identical. The eye you sharpen on the situations that cannot hurt you is the same eye you will need for the ones that can.

A note on hope in the arenas you cannot leave

Before we close, one frank word about hope, because the management strategy can sound bleak. Accepting that a relationship will not become what you hoped is a loss, and it is right to grieve it. But management is not the same as despair. People build genuinely stable, even peaceful, lives alongside a co-parent or a family member who runs the reversal, not by fixing that person, but by getting so steady in their own skills that the tactic simply has less and less to grip. The other person may not change. Your experience of them can, as your recognition sharpens, your body steadies, your records accumulate, and your support deepens. The arena you cannot leave does not have to remain as painful as it is today, even if the person in it never changes at all. That is a real and achievable kind of hope, and it is the kind this book can offer.

What to carry forward

DARVO is the same shape everywhere, because it is about escaping accountability, and that structure does not change from a bedroom to a boardroom to a courtroom (Freyd, 1997). What changes is the stakes, the tools, and whether you can leave. Every skill you have built transfers across arenas, which means you are not facing several different problems but one problem in several uniforms. In the arenas you can leave, the skills may eventually clear the way to leaving. In the arenas you cannot, the strategy shifts from resolution to management, minimizing contact, documenting, staying brief and factual, protecting your support, and accepting with grief that the relationship will not become what you hoped, so your energy goes to durable self-protection (Stark, 2007). Recognizing the tactic in public life confirms it is structural and real, not a private invention. Having seen how the reversal moves through every room of a life, we turn to the quiet, lasting damage it leaves inside you, and to the work of rebuilding trust in your own reality.

Chapter 12: Rebuilding Trust in Yourself

Valenor noticed it in a meeting that had nothing to do with any of this. They were forty-three, months past ending a long relationship built on the reversal, and a colleague simply asked what they thought of a proposal. Valenor opened their mouth and heard themselves say, well, I might be wrong, and this is probably a silly idea, but maybe, before offering a perfectly ordinary opinion. The hedging came out automatically, a reflex worn so deep they no longer felt it happening. And in that small moment Valenor understood that the relationship had ended but its residue had not. Something had been done to the way they trusted their own mind, and it had followed them out the door.

This chapter is about that residue, and about clearing it. The confrontations may end, the person may even leave your life, but DARVO leaves lasting marks on your relationship with your own reality, and healing those marks is its own distinct work. You may find yourself pre-apologizing for everything, softening every opinion, doubting your memory as a matter of habit, hearing the other person's dismissive voice in your own head. These are not permanent. They are learned patterns, installed by repetition, and what was installed by repetition can be undone by repetition of a different kind. The core injury is a loss of trust in yourself, and this chapter is about rebuilding it. That trust is the deepest thing the tactic takes, and its return is the deepest thing this book can help give back, because everything else, the recognizing and responding and documenting, finally rests on your ability to believe your own mind again.

Trust rebuilds in reps

The principle is that trust rebuilds in reps. You did not lose faith in your own mind in a single conversation, and you will not restore it in one either. It was worn down gradually, through countless small moments of having your reality denied until doubting yourself became automatic, and it comes back the same way, through countless small moments of trusting yourself and finding that trust was warranted. Recovery here is not a revelation. It is an accumulation. Each time you trust your own perception and it holds, you deposit a little evidence in favor of yourself, and over time those deposits add up to restored trust.

This matters because people expect healing to feel like a breakthrough, and when it does not, they conclude they are failing. Rebuilding self-trust rarely feels like a breakthrough. It feels like a slow, unglamorous accumulation of small moments, most of them unremarkable. That is not a sign it is not working. That is what working looks like, and knowing so keeps you from abandoning the process because it is quiet.

The pre-softening habit

The most visible residue is what Valenor caught themselves doing, the reflexive softening of every statement before it is fully out. You hedge, you qualify, you pre-apologize, you shrink your own words before anyone has even responded to them. This habit was protective once. In a relationship where raising anything plainly invited attack, softening everything in advance was a way to reduce the incoming fire. It made sense there. It makes no sense here, in the rest of your life, where it only teaches everyone, including you, that your own thoughts are things to be apologized for.

Undoing it starts with noticing it, which is why the practice at the end of this chapter begins there. Once you can hear yourself pre-soften, you can experiment with saying one thing plainly, without the cushion, and surviving the small discomfort that follows. The discomfort is real, because the cushion has felt like safety for a long time. But each time you state something plainly and nothing bad happens, you gather evidence that the plain statement is safe, and the reflex begins, slowly, to loosen its grip.

The voice in your head

One of the strangest and most painful residues of chronic DARVO is that the other person's voice can take up residence inside you, so that even in their absence you attack yourself the way they did. You raise a concern in your own mind and immediately hear, you are overreacting, you are too sensitive, you are the problem. This is not a sign that they were right. It is a sign that repetition installed their words as a track that now plays on its own, a track researchers of trauma recognize as one of the deep ways abuse persists in the body and mind long after the events (van der Kolk, 2014).

The work here is to notice the voice and, gently, to question its ownership. When the self-attacking thought arrives, you can ask, whose voice is that, really. Often you will recognize it as an echo, not your own considered judgment but a recording of someone else's tactic. Naming it as theirs begins to separate it from you, and what you can separate from you, you can eventually turn down. This is slow work, and it is helped enormously by the kind of self-compassion that meets your own struggles with warmth rather than the harshness the voice trained into you, an approach shown to support genuine healing and resilience (Neff, 2003).

Why the harsh voice is so sticky

It helps to know that you are not weak for finding the critical voice louder than the kind one. Human minds are built to weight negative information more heavily than positive, a tilt documented across a wide range of psychological research (Baumeister et al., 2001). This means the manipulator's attacks were always going to stick harder than any reassurance, and it means rebuilding a fairer inner voice takes deliberate effort against a natural headwind. You are not imagining that the cruel thoughts come more easily than the kind ones. They do, for everyone. Knowing this lets you stop treating the imbalance as further evidence of your brokenness and start treating it as a known feature of minds that you can work with, patiently, over time.

Reconnecting with your own reality

Part of rebuilding self-trust is deliberately reconnecting with the sources of reality that the tactic worked to cut you off from. This means leaning back into relationships with people who reflect the world back to you accurately, who confirm that you are not, in fact, crazy or cruel or the problem. It means paying attention to your own perceptions and treating them as data worth respecting rather than suspect testimony to be second-guessed. Recovery from this kind of harm has long been understood to depend on re-establishing safety and rebuilding a coherent, trusted sense of your own experience (Herman, 1992).

Valenor found that keeping the documentation habit from an earlier chapter served this healing too. Rereading their own contemporaneous records, written when their mind was clear, was a way of proving to themselves, over and over, that their perceptions had been accurate all along. The record did not only defend against the other person. It slowly rebuilt Valenor's faith in their own eyes, one confirmed memory at a time.

When to bring in help

This chapter, like this book, is information and support, not therapy, and some of the residue of chronic DARVO runs deep enough to warrant professional help. If you find that the self-doubt is pervasive, that the intrusive voice is relentless, that anxiety or low mood has settled in and will not lift, these are good reasons to work with a qualified therapist, ideally one who understands manipulation and trauma. Seeking that help is not a failure of the self-directed work in this book. It is an extension of it, and often the two together do what neither could alone. You do not have to rebuild everything by yourself, and for the deeper injuries, you should not have to.

Anger has a place here

Many people recovering from chronic DARVO discover, often with surprise, a wave of anger they did not expect and are not sure they are allowed to feel. For years, the tactic taught them that their anger was the problem, that objecting made them difficult, that any protest proved the other person's case. So they learned to suppress it, to be endlessly understanding, to route every feeling into self-blame instead. When that suppression finally lifts, the anger that was underneath it all can arrive with startling force, and it can be frightening if you believe anger makes you like the person who hurt you.

It does not. There is a large difference between anger that is used as a weapon to control someone and anger that is a healthy signal that a boundary was violated. Your anger, arriving now, is often the return of a faculty the tactic worked to disable, the part of you that knows when you are being wronged and says so. Recovery frequently includes reclaiming this appropriate anger, not to act it out against anyone, but to let it inform you, to let it confirm that what happened to you mattered and was not acceptable. Anger felt and understood, rather than either suppressed or vented, is a sign that your own sense of justice is coming back online. Welcome it as information, hold it without letting it run you, and let it remind you that your objections were legitimate all along.

The grief underneath

Beneath the anger there is usually grief, and it deserves its own acknowledgment, because rebuilding self-trust is not only a technical process of reps and evidence. It is also a mourning. You may be grieving the relationship you thought you had, the version of the person you believed in, the years spent doubting yourself, the self you might have been without the constant undermining. This grief is real and it is heavy, and trying to skip past it into brisk self-improvement rarely works, because the grief will wait for you until you turn toward it.

Let yourself feel it. Rebuilding trust in yourself includes grieving what the loss of that trust cost you, and the grief is not a detour from healing but part of its road. Herman's account of recovery from this kind of harm places mourning at the center of the work, not as weakness but as a necessary passage (Herman, 1992). You are allowed to be sad about what happened, sad about the time, sad about the trust, sad about the person you extended your faith to who used it against you. That sadness, fully felt, is what eventually makes room for something lighter to grow. There is no fixed timetable for this, and no one else gets to tell you that you should be over it by now. Grief moves at its own pace, and the pace is not a measure of your progress. Give it the room it asks for, and trust that feeling it through is faster, in the end, than forcing it down.

The relief when certainty returns

There is a quiet reward at the far end of this work, and it is worth holding out to yourself as you go, because the early stages are slow and can feel thankless. As the reps accumulate, a day arrives when someone denies something you know to be true and you simply do not wobble. You feel the old pull toward self-doubt, recognize it, and let it pass, because your trust in your own mind has become sturdier than the pull. Valenor described the first time it happened as a kind of stillness, a strange and welcome quiet where the frantic self-checking used to be.

That stillness is what you are building toward. Not the ability to win arguments, not the power to change the other person, but the simple, steady, unshakeable knowledge of what is real, held so securely that no denial can dislodge it. It comes gradually and then, one ordinary day, you notice it has arrived. When it does, you will understand that the point of all this work was never to defeat anyone. It was to come home to your own mind and be able, finally, to trust what you find there.

Trying it on your own life

The practice here is gentle and cumulative, because self-trust is rebuilt gently and cumulatively.

First, spend one week simply noticing your pre-softening, without forcing yourself to stop. Mark each time you hedge, qualify, or pre-apologize before offering an ordinary thought. Awareness comes before change, and you cannot loosen a reflex you have not yet learned to hear.

Second, once a day, say one thing plainly, without the cushion. A preference, an opinion, a small need, stated without hedging or apology. Notice that the discomfort passes and nothing bad happens. Each plain statement is a rep, a small deposit of evidence that your own words are safe to say.

Third, when the harsh inner voice speaks, practice asking, whose voice is that, and answering squarely. When you recognize an echo of the other person's tactic, name it as theirs, not yours. Then, deliberately, offer yourself the sentence a kind friend would say instead. You are not silencing the voice by force. You are slowly building a fairer one beside it, and over time the fairer one grows louder.

Fourth, keep a short running list of moments when you trusted your own perception and were proven right. When you sensed something was off and it turned out to be, when you remembered an event accurately and later found confirmation, when your read of a situation held up. Add to it whenever such a moment occurs. This list is a growing body of evidence in your own favor, assembled deliberately to counter the years of evidence the tactic manufactured against you. On the hard days, when the old self-doubt rises, you can read it, and it will remind you, in your own documented words, that your mind has been trustworthy more often than the reversal ever let you believe. You are, in the most literal sense, rebuilding the case for yourself, one entry at a time.

Where this leaves you

DARVO leaves residue, a loss of trust in your own reality that outlasts the relationship, showing up as pre-softening, chronic self-doubt, and the other person's dismissive voice playing in your own head (van der Kolk, 2014). None of it is permanent, because what repetition installed, a different repetition can undo. Trust rebuilds in reps, through the slow accumulation of small moments in which you trust yourself and find that trust warranted. You loosen the pre-softening habit by noticing it and speaking plainly, you separate the harsh inner voice from your own by naming it as an echo, you work against the natural stickiness of criticism with deliberate self-compassion (Neff, 2003; Baumeister et al., 2001), and you reconnect with the people and records that reflect reality back accurately (Herman, 1992). Where the injury runs deep, a good therapist is an extension of this work, not a replacement for your effort. With your recognition sharp, your responses ready, and your self-trust rebuilding, one thing remains, to gather all of it into a single plan you can actually carry into your life. That is the final chapter.

Chapter 13: The Plan You Carry

Alaris made a discovery that changed how she used everything she had learned. She was thirty-six, and she had read widely, understood the tactic deeply, and could explain DARVO to anyone who asked. Yet in the moment, facing her mother-in-law across a kitchen table, all of that knowledge scattered like startled birds, and she reached for none of it. The problem was not that she did not know what to do. The problem was that her knowledge lived in a hundred scattered pieces, and a flooded moment is no time to assemble a hundred pieces. What she needed was not more understanding. She needed one page, simple enough to hold under pressure, that gathered the essentials into something she could actually reach for.

That one page is what this final chapter builds. Everything in this book, recognition, regulation, response, documentation, self-trust, comes together here into a personal plan you can carry into your life and use before your hardest conversations. A plan you read and set down helps for a week. A plan you carry helps for years, because it turns scattered knowledge into a single reachable tool. This chapter walks you through assembling yours, section by section, so that when the reversal comes, you are not trying to remember thirteen chapters. You are reaching for one page you have already made.

The plan you carry

The principle of this chapter is simply the plan you carry. Knowledge that stays in a book, or scattered across your memory, is not available when you are flooded and the reversal is underway. A plan works because it does the assembling in advance, in calm, so that the flooded version of you has to do almost nothing except follow steps already laid down. The best plan is short, personal, and specific to the person and situation you actually face, because a general plan is just more knowledge to sift through, while a specific plan is a tool you can grab. We will build yours in six parts, each drawn from a skill you already have.

Part one, your recognition cues

The plan begins with how you, specifically, know the reversal is starting. Everyone has particular tells, both in the other person's behavior and in their own body. Write down the signs that DARVO is beginning with this person: the phrases they tend to use, the way the conversation characteristically turns, and your own physical signals, the tight chest, the hot face, the urge to prove or to apologize. These cues are your early warning system, and naming them in advance means you catch the tactic sooner, when you still have the most room to respond well. Recognition is the foundation everything else rests on, so it comes first.

Part two, your regulation move

Next, write down the single regulation practice you will use when you notice the cues, chosen and already rehearsed. For most people this is the long exhale, out longer than in, repeated a few times. Name yours specifically, so that in the moment you are not deciding what to do but executing something decided. Add your grounding technique if you use one, and your pause sentence, the exact words you will say to buy time: I need a minute, or let me think about that and come back to you. This part of the plan ensures that before you try to respond, you steady the body that has to do the responding.

Part three, your two go-to lines

Now the words. From the scripts you developed earlier, choose the two you are most likely to need with this person, written in your own voice. Not all of them, just two, because two you can actually remember and reach for. Perhaps one line that holds your point and one that declines the fight, or one that refuses the role and one that lets you leave cleanly. Whichever two fit your situation, write them exactly as you would say them. These are the sentences you reach for when your mind goes blank, and having only two, ready and rehearsed, serves you far better than knowing all of them vaguely.

Part four, your documentation habit

Write down how and where you will keep your record. Name the place, a specific note, a private document, an email to yourself, that the other person cannot access. Decide your trigger, that you will write a factual account as soon as possible after any significant exchange with this person. Making this concrete in the plan means the habit actually happens, rather than remaining a good intention. The record, as you know, protects both your standing and your grip on reality, and a plan that names exactly where and when you will keep it is a plan that gets kept.

Part five, your support and your exit

Write down two things here. First, your anchor people, the specific names of those whose knowledge of you can withstand a false story, and a commitment to reach toward them rather than withdraw when things are hard. Second, your exit criteria, the moment at which you will disengage from a given conversation, decided in advance: when the loop repeats, when the attack turns to your character, whenever you choose. Deciding your exit point in calm means you are not trying to make that judgment while flooded, and naming your anchors in advance means you know exactly where to turn when the isolation the tactic seeks starts to bite.

Part six, your reality reminder

Finally, write one sentence that returns you to yourself, a line you can read when the reversal has you doubting everything. It might be their tactic working is not proof that I am wrong. It might be I know what happened, and I do not need them to agree. It might be my reality is mine to trust. Choose the sentence that steadies you most, and put it at the bottom of the plan, so that whatever else happens, you close on solid ground. This is the reminder that all the skills serve one purpose, keeping you in possession of your own reality (Harsey & Freyd, 2020).

Using the plan

A plan works only if you use it, so build the habit of reading it before conversations you know will be hard. Before the family dinner, the co-parenting handoff, the difficult meeting, take one minute to read your page. You are pre-loading yourself, moving the plan from paper into readiness, so that the flooded version of you finds the steps already familiar. Update it as you learn. After each hard encounter, notice what worked and what you would change, and revise the plan accordingly, so it grows sharper and more yours over time. Herman's understanding of recovery emphasizes the restoration of a sense of power and control (Herman, 1992), and a plan you built and refine is exactly that, your own agency, made concrete and portable.

Watching the plan work

It helps to see a plan in motion, so return to Alaris at that kitchen table. This time she has her page, and she read it in the car before walking in. When her mother-in-law denies having said something Alaris clearly remembers, Alaris feels her chest tighten, which is on her page as a recognition cue, so instead of scrambling to prove the point she takes two long exhales, which is her regulation move. When the denial turns into an attack on how Alaris runs her household, she does not defend, because part four of her plan reminds her not to. She reaches for one of her two go-to lines, said flatly: that is not what we are talking about right now. When the attack becomes a wounded performance about how unwelcome her mother-in-law feels, Alaris recognizes the reversal, declines the role, and, as the loop begins to repeat, uses her exit: I think we should leave this here for now. Afterward, in the car again, she writes down what was said while it is fresh.

Nothing about that evening was a triumph in the ordinary sense. Alaris did not win, did not extract an apology, did not change her mother-in-law at all. But she moved through the entire reversal without losing her footing, without confessing to things she had not done, and without the hours of afterward self-doubt that used to follow. The difference was not that she knew more than before. She knew exactly the same things. The difference was that the knowledge was on one page she could reach, instead of scattered across a mind that scattered further the moment she was flooded. That is the whole case for the plan, made concrete.

What a finished plan can look like

To make this tangible, here is the shape a completed one-page plan might take, in brief. Under recognition cues: she says that never happened in a flat, certain voice; my chest tightens and I want to grab my phone to prove things. Under regulation move: three long exhales, out for eight; if needed, the sentence let me think about that for a second. Under my two lines: that is the thing I want to talk about, and that has not changed, and I am not going to argue about my character. Under documentation: I write what was said in my private notes app within an hour, dated. Under support and exit: I call my sister, who knows me; I leave when the same denial comes a second time. Under reality reminder: I know what happened, and I do not need them to agree.

Yours will look different, because yours will fit your person and your situation, and it should. The point is not to copy this one but to see how little a working plan actually contains. Six short parts, one page, entirely reachable. You do not need more than that. In fact, more than that would defeat the purpose, because the plan's power comes precisely from being small enough to hold when everything in you is scattering.

When the plan does not go perfectly

A final truth, because plans and books can imply a tidiness that real life does not have. There will be times when you read your plan, walk in prepared, and still get caught. The reversal will find an angle you did not expect, or you will be too tired or too triggered that day to execute, and you will leave having apologized or exploded or frozen despite everything. This will happen. It is not a failure of the plan and it is not a failure of you.

When it happens, the move is the same one this whole book has been teaching in a hundred forms: return to your ground, without self-attack. Notice what caught you, add it to your plan, and let the difficult encounter become information rather than evidence against yourself. Progress in this work is not a straight line from caught to free. It is a gradual shift in the ratio, more encounters where you hold your footing, fewer where you lose it, over months and years. A single bad conversation does not erase that progress any more than a single good one completes it. You are building something durable, and durable things are built unevenly, with setbacks folded in. The plan is not a promise that you will never be caught again. It is a way of being caught less often, recovering faster, and always, always having a way back to your own ground.

One last thought on why the plan matters more than any single skill in it. Throughout this book, the reversal has depended on catching you unprepared, on arriving faster than your thinking, on finding you without a ready response. The plan is the answer to all of that at once. It is preparation made portable, thinking done in advance so it does not have to be done under fire, a response made ready before it is needed. When you carry it, you change the fundamental conditions of every hard conversation, because you are no longer improvising against a practiced tactic. You are meeting a practiced tactic with a practiced response of your own. That shift, from improvising to prepared, is quietly the difference between the person you were at the start of this book and the person you are now.

Trying it on your own life

The practice for this final chapter is to build your plan, and it is the most important single action in the book.

First, sit down in a calm moment and write all six parts on one page, in your own words, specific to the person you most often face. Recognition cues, regulation move, two go-to lines, documentation habit, support and exit, and reality reminder. Keep it to a single page, because a page you can hold is worth more than an essay you cannot.

Second, put the plan somewhere you can reach it fast, a note on your phone, a card in your wallet, and read it once before your next hard conversation. The reading is what turns the plan from a document into a readiness.

Third, after your next encounter, revise the plan based on what you learned. This makes it a living tool that sharpens with use, and it makes you an active builder of your own protection rather than a passive reader of someone else's advice.

Fourth, share the fact of your plan, though not necessarily its contents, with one of your anchor people. Simply telling someone who supports you that you have made a plan for handling these conversations does two useful things. It creates a small accountability that helps you actually use it, and it enlists an ally who can remind you, when you are wobbling, that you have a tool and a way through. You do not have to show them the page. You only have to let one trusted person know that you are no longer walking into these conversations unarmed and alone, which is itself a quiet act of the self-respect this entire book has been building toward.

What to carry forward

Knowledge scattered across thirteen chapters is not available in a flooded moment, but a single page is, and that is the plan you carry. Built in calm from the skills you already have, it gathers your recognition cues, your regulation move, your two go-to lines, your documentation habit, your support and exit, and your reality reminder into one reachable tool. Read before hard conversations and revised after them, it becomes your own agency made portable, the restoration of power and control that recovery depends on (Herman, 1992). You began this book walking in wronged and walking out apologizing, without even a word for what was happening. You end it with a name for the tactic, an understanding of why it works, a self-check that keeps you grounded, the skills to recognize and respond and document and withstand and heal, and now a plan to hold it all. What remains is the shortest and truest instruction in the book, and it is the one the whole series is named around. Name the tactic. Reclaim your reality.

Conclusion: Name the Tactic, Reclaim Your Reality

Think back to the moment this book began, the one you were probably living when you picked it up. You went in to say one true thing, and you came out apologizing, unsure how it happened, carrying a question that pointed straight at yourself. What is wrong with me. You did not have a word for the thing that had just been done to you, and without a word, the confusion had nowhere to go but inward.

Look at how much has changed. You have a word now, and behind the word a whole structure you can see: deny, attack, reverse victim and offender, three moves with three jobs, running in an order designed to leave you exactly where you kept ending up. You understand why it worked on you, not because you are weak or foolish, but because the tactic grips people precisely by their fairness, their empathy, and their willingness to believe they might be wrong. What felt like proof of your defectiveness turns out to be evidence of a tactic doing what tactics do.

You have more than understanding. You have a way to stay clear-eyed, the accountability check that keeps this from becoming a label you hide behind, so that your recognition is something you can trust and others can respect. You have the difference between DARVO and gaslighting and ordinary defensiveness, so you can name the right thing and answer it rightly. You have the first and most important response, steadying your own body before you speak, and the six responses that hold your ground once you are steady, and the actual words to reach for when your mind would otherwise go blank. You have the record that outlasts the doubt, the way through the smear when the reversal goes public, the map of how the same shape appears in every arena, the slow rebuilding of trust in your own reality, and finally the plan that gathers all of it onto one page you can carry.

Let me be upfront about what this book has not given you, because straight talk is what separates real help from false comfort. It has not given you a way to change the other person. No book can, and any that promises to is selling something. It has not given you a magic sentence that stops a determined manipulator, because that sentence does not exist. It has not promised that everyone will believe the truth, or that the relationships strained by a reversal will all survive, or that the road ahead is short. These would be lies, and you have had enough of those.

What it has given you is the only thing that was ever actually in your power, and it turns out to be enough. You cannot control what another person does, but you can keep your footing while they do it. You cannot make anyone see the truth, but you can hold onto it yourself, so securely that no denial can take it from you. You cannot guarantee the outcome of any conversation, but you can walk out of it with your reality and your dignity intact, which, as you now know, is the victory that was always available and the only one you needed.

There is a particular freedom in this, and it deserves naming as we close. For a long time, your peace depended on something you could not control, on whether the other person would finally admit the truth, take responsibility, stop. As long as your peace waited on their change, you were captive, because their change was never coming. The work of this book moves the ground of your peace from them to you, from their behavior, which you cannot control, to your own footing, which you can. That is what it means to reclaim your reality. It is not winning against them. It is ceasing to need to.

The tactic depends on the dark, on your not being able to name what is happening, on the confusion that has nowhere to go but inward. You have turned on the light. The three moves that once swept you away are now three moves you can watch, name, and answer. That does not make the people who use them disappear, and it does not make the hard conversations easy. But it changes who you are inside them, from someone lost in a fog they could not name to someone standing, steady, on ground they know is theirs.

You began without a word. You end with a name, an understanding, a set of skills, and a plan. Whatever comes next, in whatever arena, with whomever runs the reversal, you carry the one thing the tactic was built to take from you and could not. You know what is real. Hold onto it. Name the tactic, and reclaim your reality.

Appendix A: The DARVO Response Card

Keep this where you can reach it fast. Read it before conversations you know will be hard.

Recognition. Deny (that never happened), Attack (you are the problem), Reverse (I am the real victim). When the subject drifts from what they did to who you are, that is the reversal.

My body's cues. Tight chest, hot face, the urge to prove, the urge to apologize. These signal the tactic before my mind names it.

Regulate first. Breathe out longer than in, three times. Ground my feet. Say: let me think about that for a moment.

Hold the ground. Name it inside: this is DARVO. Do not defend the reversal. Restate my issue once, flatly. Refuse the role of villain. Disengage when the loop repeats. Bring a witness when I can.

My two lines. ____.
And: ____.

Reality reminder. Their tactic working is not proof I am wrong. I know what happened. My reality is mine to trust.

Appendix B: The Documentation Log

Use one entry per significant exchange. Write as soon as possible afterward, while it is fresh. Keep it somewhere the other person cannot access.

Date and time: ____________________

What I raised, and why: ____________________

What was said, in order (their words and mine, as close to exact as I can recall): ____________________

How it ended: ____________________

My experience, kept separate from the facts above (how I felt, what I doubted): ____________________

Keep entries factual. Record observations (she said the money was never there), not conclusions (she lied). Store them dated and safe.

Appendix C: The Is-This-DARVO Self-Check

Run these before concluding that a conflict is a reversal rather than a legitimate confrontation.

1. Am I genuinely open to the possibility that I am wrong here?

2. Is the other person raising something specific that I actually did, rather than attacking my character to dodge a topic?

3. Does the fault always, without exception, land on them and never on me?

4. If I grant their point for a moment, would it cost me only discomfort, or would it require denying something I directly witnessed?

If the label survives a searching run through these questions, you can trust it. If it does not, you have learned something more useful than a confirmation. Remember: being manipulated and being wrong can both be true at once.

Appendix D: Weak Line to Strong Line

Weak lines defend, plead, or escalate, and hand back control. Strong lines are short, flat, and return you to your ground. Rewrite these in your own voice.

Weak: I am not controlling, why would you even say that. Strong: I am not going to argue about my character.

Weak: Please just admit what you did, why can you not see it. Strong: What I raised is the thing I want to talk about.

Weak: After everything I have done for you, how dare you. Strong: I am not the one who caused harm here, and I am not going to act as if I am.

Weak: Fine, I give up, this is pointless, you always win. Strong: I have said what I needed to. I am going to stop here.

Appendix E: Going Deeper, The DARVO Survival Guides

This book is the hub of a series. If your situation fits one of these arenas, a dedicated guide goes further than a single chapter can.

The DARVO Decoder is for documenting a manipulative ex through divorce, custody, and co-parenting.

Named as the Abuser is for reactive-abuse survivors who reacted to harm and were then cast as the abuser.

DARVO at Work is for handling the deny-attack-reverse tactic from a manipulative boss or colleague.

When You Became the Villain is for adult children of a parent who denied, attacked, and made them the bad guy.

Wherever the tactic is showing up in your life, there is a book built for exactly that situation. Name the tactic. Reclaim your reality.

References

Baumeister, R. F., Bratslavsky, E., Finkenauer, C., & Vohs, K. D. (2001). Bad is stronger than good. *Review of General Psychology, 5*(4), 323-370. https://doi.org/10.1037/1089-2680.5.4.323

Freyd, J. J. (1996). *Betrayal trauma: The logic of forgetting childhood abuse*. Harvard University Press.

Freyd, J. J. (1997). Violations of power, adaptive blindness, and betrayal trauma theory. *Feminism & Psychology, 7*(1), 22-32. https://doi.org/10.1177/0959353597071004

Harsey, S. J., & Freyd, J. J. (2020). Deny, attack, and reverse victim and offender (DARVO): What is the influence on perceived perpetrator and victim credibility? *Journal of Aggression, Maltreatment & Trauma, 29*(8), 897-916. https://doi.org/10.1080/10926771.2020.1774695

Harsey, S. J., Zurbriggen, E. L., & Freyd, J. J. (2017). Perpetrator responses to victim confrontation: DARVO and victim self-blame. *Journal of Aggression, Maltreatment & Trauma, 26*(6), 644-663. https://doi.org/10.1080/10926771.2017.1320777

Herman, J. L. (1992). *Trauma and recovery*. Basic Books.

Neff, K. D. (2003). Self-compassion: An alternative conceptualization of a healthy attitude toward oneself. *Self and Identity, 2*(2), 85-101. https://doi.org/10.1080/15298860309032

Porges, S. W. (2011). *The polyvagal theory: Neurophysiological foundations of emotions, attachment, communication, and self-regulation*. W. W. Norton.

Smith, C. P., & Freyd, J. J. (2014). Institutional betrayal. *American Psychologist, 69*(6), 575-587. https://doi.org/10.1037/a0037564

Stark, E. (2007). *Coercive control: How men entrap women in personal life*. Oxford University Press.

Sweet, P. L. (2019). The sociology of gaslighting. *American Sociological Review, 84*(5), 851-875. https://doi.org/10.1177/0003122419874843

van der Kolk, B. A. (2014). *The body keeps the score: Brain, mind, and body in the healing of trauma*. Viking.

About Author

Arnold Wellington McLean is a mental health professional and researcher with an interest in trauma. His work focuses on how manipulation and betrayal affect the people subjected to them, and on turning that understanding into plain, practical guidance. He is the author of The DARVO Survival Guides, a series that helps readers name the deny, attack, reverse tactic and respond to it with clarity and self-respect.

www.ingramcontent.com/pod-product-compliance
Lightning Source LLC
LaVergne TN
LVHW050825061126
851857LV00012B/980
* 9 7 9 8 9 0 6 7 8 2 2 0 5 *